FILTHY RICH

VERTIGO CRIME

WRITER
BRIAN AZZARELLO

ART
VICTOR SANTOS

LETTERS
CLEM ROBINS

FILTHY RICH

FILTHY RICH
VERTIGO CRIME

ONCE UPON A TIME...

THAT'S HOW A GOOD STORY **STARTS,** RIGHT?...

NO, ONCE UPON A TIME...

...IS HOW A **FAIRY TALE** BEGINS...

FOLLOWED BY THERE WAS A HANDSOME PRINCE, THAT EVERYONE *LOVED.*

...THAT WOULD BE ME.

SO THIS PRINCE, HE WAS...*PRINCELY*. AND HE...LOVED THE PEOPLE WHO LOVED HIM BACK.

HE DID EVERYTHING IN HIS POWER TO SHOW THIS TO THEM, SO THEY'D LOVE HIM EVEN MORE.

AND THEY *DID*. BECAUSE THEY KNEW, JUST LIKE THE PRINCE, THAT HE WAS DESTINED TO DO GREAT THINGS.

BUT THEN LIKE IN *EVERY* ONE OF THESE STORIES, SOMETHING CAME OUT OF NOWHERE, AND FUCKED IT ALL *UP*. SO THE PRINCE?...

MY LIFE *ENDED* THREE YEARS AGO.

IT WASN'T A *SPECTACULAR* DEATH BY ANY MEANS, JUST A LITTLE *"POP."*

6

AND THEN IT WAS *OVER*.

IT'S NOT *EASY* KNOWING YOUR PRINCE DAYS ARE *BEHIND* YOU. I MEAN, WHEN THAT REALIZATION COMES...

THE THOUGHTS ARE...*DARK*.

VERY DARK. LIKE WHAT YER THINKIN'...

...ARE THE *LAST* THOUGHTS YOU'LL EVER *HAVE*.

BUT THEN SOMETHING *HAPPENS*...

Meadow Gold
MILK ICE CREAM

THE SUN KEEPS COMING UP...

AND LIFE GOES ON.

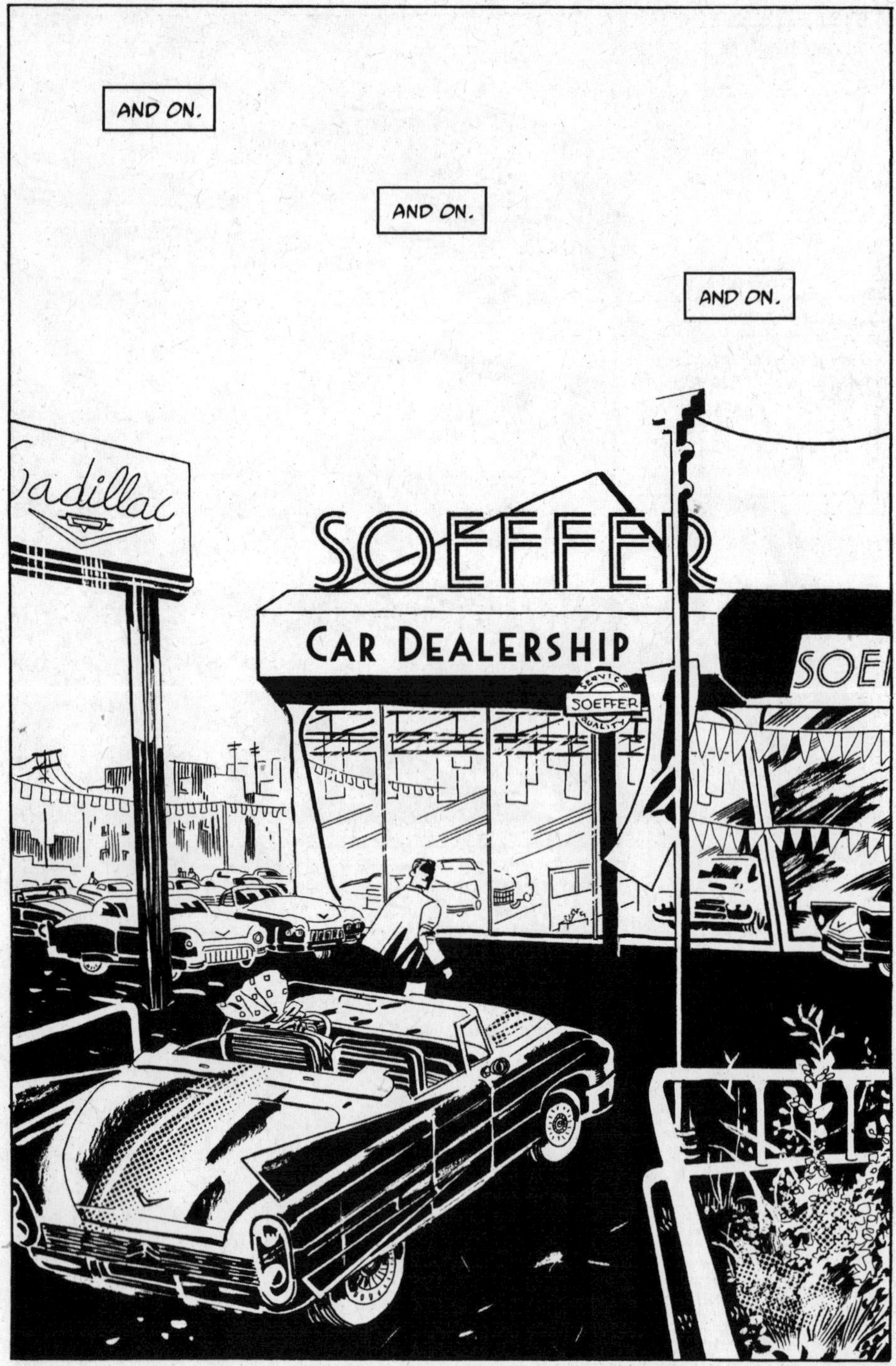
AND ON.
AND ON.
AND ON.
Cadillac
SOEFFER
CAR DEALERSHIP
SERVICE
SOEFFER
QUALITY
SOE

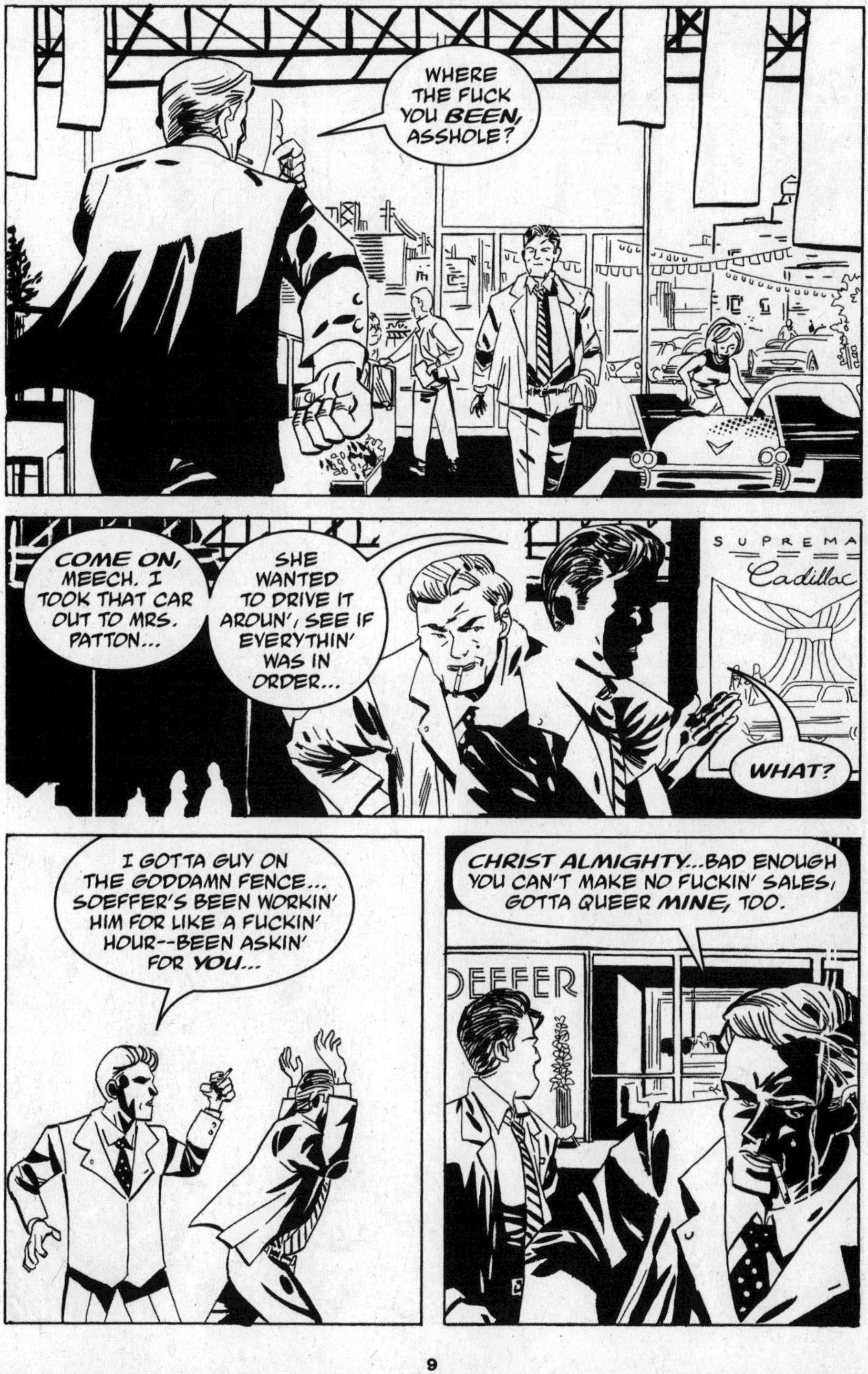
WHERE THE FUCK YOU BEEN, ASSHOLE?
COME ON, MEECH. I TOOK THAT CAR OUT TO MRS. PATTON...
SHE WANTED TO DRIVE IT AROUN', SEE IF EVERYTHIN' WAS IN ORDER...
SUPREMA
Cadillac
WHAT?
I GOTTA GUY ON THE GODDAMN FENCE... SOEFFER'S BEEN WORKIN' HIM FOR LIKE A FUCKIN' HOUR--BEEN ASKIN' FOR YOU...
CHRIST ALMIGHTY...BAD ENOUGH YOU CAN'T MAKE NO FUCKIN' SALES, GOTTA QUEER MINE, TOO.
OEFFER

--I THINK I BETTER *THINK* ABOUT IT.

THAT'S SMART, MR. ROBERTS-- *VERY* SMART. YOU SHOULD TREAT THIS DECISION NOT LIKE BUYING A CAR, BUT MAKING A SOUND INVESTMENT...

I NEED YOU TO MAKE ME A PROMISE. I NEED YOU TO PROMISE ME THAT YOU WON'T TAKE MY PRICE DOWN THE ROAD TO ANOTHER DEALER, BECAUSE THE PRICE... IF THE MANUFACTURER FOUND OUT...

THEY WOULD **NOT** BE HAPPY WITH THIS PRICE I'M GIVING YOU.

MR. SOEFFER, I JUST GOT BACK FROM MRS. PATTON'S, AND SHE TOLD ME TO THANK YOU FOR THE SERVICE WE PERFORMED ON HER--

I'M SORRY, SIR. I DIDN'T KNOW YOU WERE WITH A CUSTOMER...

THAT'S OKAY, RICH. I'M **ALWAYS** GLAD TO HEAR ABOUT A SATISFIED CUSTOMER.

SAY, ROBERTS, YOU FOLLOW FOOTBALL? REMEMBER THIS GUY?

RICH *JUNKIN?*

THAT'S RIGHT. MISTER FOOTBALL NEW JERSEY NINETEEN FIFTY-FOUR.

NO, IT WAS FIFTY-*FIVE*, WASN'T IT?

I AIN'T A FAN OF THE GAME. BUT HE WAS THE BEST HIGH SCHOOL PLAYER IN THE STATE.

DAMN *STRAIGHT* HE WAS!

THEN THREE TIME ALL-AMERICAN AT NOTRE DAME. *THREE TIME!*

DRAFTED FIRST ROUND BY *CLEVELAND,* WASN'T IT?

YES SIR.

HAD THE WORLD BY THE SHORT HAIRS, THIS ONE DID--EVEN WITH THEM COCKAMAMIE ALLEGATIONS THE *FEDS* WERE MAKIN'. I MEAN, THE IRISH DIDN'T LOSE A GAME THAT YEAR, SO HOW COULD THEY BE *TRUE?*

JUST A FIST FULL OF SHORT HAIRS... AND THEN...

YOU MIND? SHOWIN' US YER *SCAR?*

BLINDSIDED. THE LAST PRE-SEASON GAME HIS ROOKIE YEAR. DOWN HE WENT...

...NEVER TO PLAY A DOWN IN THE PROS.

YEAH, I KNOW... WHAT A TOUGH BREAK.

TOUGH BREAK? THIS MAN WOULDA MADE THE HALL OF FAME--A FUCKING TRAGEDY'S WHAT IT IS--PARDON MY FRENCH.

HEY JUNK, I NEVER BELIEVED ANY OF THAT STUFF I READ IN THE PAPERS ABOUT YOU.

--YOU THINK I DID? YOU THINK I WOULD HIRE THAT TYPE OF GUY TO WORK FOR ME?

THAT'S NOT THE KIND OF BUSINESS I RUN.

HERB SOEFFER IS AN HONEST MAN. I WANT YOU TO KNOW THAT--EVEN IF YOU DECIDE TO MAKE YOUR INVESTMENT WITH ANOTHER DEALER.

FAT CHANCE A' THAT-- WE HAD HIM...

14

...BY THE SHORT HAIRS. THE BOSS HEMMED AND HAWED, THEN SAID HE WOULD EAT THE HUNDRED DOLLAR PREP CHARGE-- BECAUSE ROBERTS WAS A *FAN* OF MINE.

WHILE I REGALED HIM WITH BULLSHIT OF MY "GRIDIRON GLORY," MR. ROBERTS SIGNED THE PAPERS AND BECAME THE OWNER OF ONE OF THE MOST EXPENSIVE CARS ON THE *LOT*.

AND HE WAS *HAPPY* ABOUT IT BECAUSE HE BELIEVED HE GOT A DEAL--THAT HE WAS ABLE TO GET THE BEST PRICE--BLEED US DOWN TO OUR LAST *NICKEL*-- AND COULD TELL HIS FRIENDS...

"I GOT A GREAT DEAL." THAT'S MORE IMPORTANT THAN SELLING A *CAR* IN THIS GAME...

THE *ONLY* GAME I WAS IN NOW.

HOW'S THE SANDWICH?

MMM.

MMM MMM

SO BABY...

I'M NOT *WORKING* MONDAY NIGHT.

OH YEAH?

YEAH. TUESDAY'S *YOUR* DAY OFF, RIGHT?

UH HUH.

I THOUGHT MAYBE WE COULD GO TO THE SHORE.

WHADDYA MEAN *MAYBE*, CHARLENE?...

IF YOU DON' HAVETA WORK MONDAY NIGHT, WE *GO.*

I'LL PICK YOU UP, RIGHT AFTER I GET OFF. WE CAN HAVE DINNER AT THAT PLACE YOU LIKE--

--OR A PICNIC ON THE BEACH--YOU CAN BUILD A FIRE.

THAT SOUNDS GREAT, REALLY GREAT. IT'LL BE NICE TO GET OUT OF TOWN, EVEN FOR JUST A NIGHT AND A DAY.

WE'LL HAVE A SWELL TIME, RICH, A SWELL TIME.

YOU AND ME ALWAYS DO, CHARLENE.

ALWAYS.

HEY JUNK--

WHAT YOU WANT, VINNY JUNIOR?

I NEED TO KNOW WHAT YOU THINK OF THIS NUMBER...

I THINK IT'S A THREE.

YOU THINK YOU CAN *BEAT* IT?

S'A *BET*...THE OVER/UNDER ON HOW MANY *JALOPIES* YOU GONNA MOVE THIS WEEKEND.

MY MONEY'S ON THE UNDER-- *KEEP* IT THAT WAY...

I'LL CUT YOU *IN.*

HA HAHAHAHA

RICH, *NO!*--

VINNY CAMPOZZO JUNIOR WAS A GRADE-A *DICKWEED.*

I HATED HIM, AND GUYS LIKE HIM.

SMART ALECK SHITS WHO *LIVED* TO GET UNDER MY SKIN.

DON'T WORRY, CHARLENE...

I'M JUST CALLIN' IT A NIGHT. I GOTTA GET AN EARLY START AT THE *LOT...*

HEY FELLAS!

BET THE *OVER.*

BET THE OVER?

WASN'T THE *FIRST* TIME I'D GIVEN A BUM STEER.

LOST ANOTHER ONE, JUNK?

WAS A LOUSY UP, JERRY--THEY WERE JUST LOOKING.

JUNK, HOW MANY TIMES I GOTTA TELL YOU: NO ONE--*NO* ONE-- STEPS ON A LOT TO JUST LOOK. THEY WERE HERE TO *BUY.*

THEY WANT A *CAR.* YOUR JOB IS TO MAKE THEM HAPPY TO *PAY* FOR IT.

MAYBE I AIN'T CUT *OUT* FOR THIS.

YOU MIGHT BE RIGHT.

HELLO BOYS, HOW'S THE MORNING BEEN?

THEY WERE ASKIN' ON YOU, MEECH.

WHO?

STAR OF THE WEEK

OFFER!

EASIEST SALE I EVER MADE.

HARDY HAR HAR.

BOSS IN?

NOT YET.

WELL, HE'S GONNA HAVE A CANNON UP HIS ASS WHEN HE *DOES* GET HERE-- THAT LITTLE *GIRL* A' HIS MADE THE PAPERS-- AGAIN.

OH BOY.

SERIOUSLY, EITHER OF YOU MOVE *ANYTHING* YET?

TWO? MY DEAR, AND IT'S NOT EVEN *LUNCH* TIME.

IT IS FOR ME.

I HEADED DOWN TO PUP'S TAP, FOR A SAUSAGE AND A BEER. THE MORNING HAD BEEN A COMPLETE CRAP OUT, JUST ONE BAD UP AFTER *ANOTHER*, WHILE THE REST OF THE GUYS WERE MAKIN' THEIR NUTS.

USUALLY, I'D WRITE THAT OFF AS THE KIND OF STREAK EVERY GUY HITS ONCE IN A WHILE AND I WOULDN'T LET IT BOTHER ME--BUT IT WAS FEELING LIKE SOMETHING *MORE*.

IT WAS FEELING LIKE IT WAS THE WAY THINGS WERE FOR ME. AND *WOULD* BE. AS IF LIFE WAS SAYING, "THIS IS ALL I *GOT LEFT* FOR YOU, JUNK."

IT DIDN'T HELP MATTERS THAT PUP WAS GIVIN' ME THE BUSINESS FOR DRINKING ON MY LUNCH HOUR, LIKE I WAS SOME THIRD SHIFT *LOSER* MARKING MY TIME WITH EVERY SIP I TOOK.

ABOUT HALFWAY THROUGH THE GLASS, I WAS FEELIN' BETTER--AND A LITTLE *ASHAMED*. LIFE DIDN'T HAVE IT IN FOR ME--IT WAS JUST BAD LUCK, AND I PROMISED MYSELF THAT STARTING THAT AFTERNOON...

JUST TO SHOW HIM HE WASN'T *GETTIN'* TO ME, I ORDERED ANOTHER BEER.

...I'D TURN IT *AROUND.*

KNOCK KNOCK

YES?

OH...MR. MILLS. I WASN'T EXPECTING--

CAN I *HELP* YOU?

I'M SORRY, SIR...I'M FROM SOEFFER MOTORS. I DROPPED OFF A CAR A FEW WEEKS AGO TO YOUR *WIFE*--

OH, YES, YES--

--I WAS IN THE NEIGHBORHOOD...THIS IS JUST A COURTESY CALL, MAKIN' SURE EVERYTHING'S *FINE.*

OH. WELL, YES, OF *COURSE* IT IS, SON. I MEAN, IF IT WASN'T?...

...YOU WOULD HAVE *HEARD* FROM ME.

RIGHT, SIR. OKAY, THAT'S GREAT. I'LL BE ON MY WAY, THEN...

THANK YOU FOR STOPPING BY--AND YOU TELL BOB MEECHUM THAT WHEN I'M IN THE MARKET FOR MY NEXT CAR, I'LL LOOK HIM UP.

YES, SIR...

"...I'LL DO THAT."

HEY FELLAS, LOOK WHO IT IS--THE MAN OF THE HOUR...

Cadillac Quality

OR SHOULD I SAY EXTRA LONG LUNCH HOUR.

NOT A GOOD DAY FOR RELAXING, JUNK.

C'MON, I WAS WORKIN' A LEAD, JERRY...

COUPLE CAME IN THE OTHER DAY, SO I STOPPED BY THEIR PLACE, INVITED THEM BACK FOR A TEST DRIVE.

HAH! THE AMOUNT A' BULLSHIT THAT COMES OUTTA THIS MOUTH...

MEANS THIS NOSE IS VERY FAMILIAR WITH THE SCENT. YOU GOT A SECRET...

AN' I KNOW WHAT IT IS.

LAY OFF, MEECH. I GOT **NO** SECRETS.

TSK, TSK. YOU **DISAPPOINT** ME, JUNK OLD KID. NOT WILLING TO LEVEL WITH YER BUDDIES, HUH? THAT'S OKAY...

I'LL DO IT. GENTS--

...KEEP IT TO **YERSELF**, MEECH, YOU KNOW WHAT'S **GOOD** FOR YOU...

--I GOT THE **REAL SKINNY** ON OUR BOY JUNK HERE. SOMETHIN' HE'S BEEN **HIDIN'** FROM US.

HE MUST BE A **SHY** ONE-- I DON' KNOW WHY, BECAUSE IF **I** WAS HIM, I'D BE **BRAGGIN'** THAT I WAS--

Cadillac Quality

...INDEPENDENTLY WEALTHY.

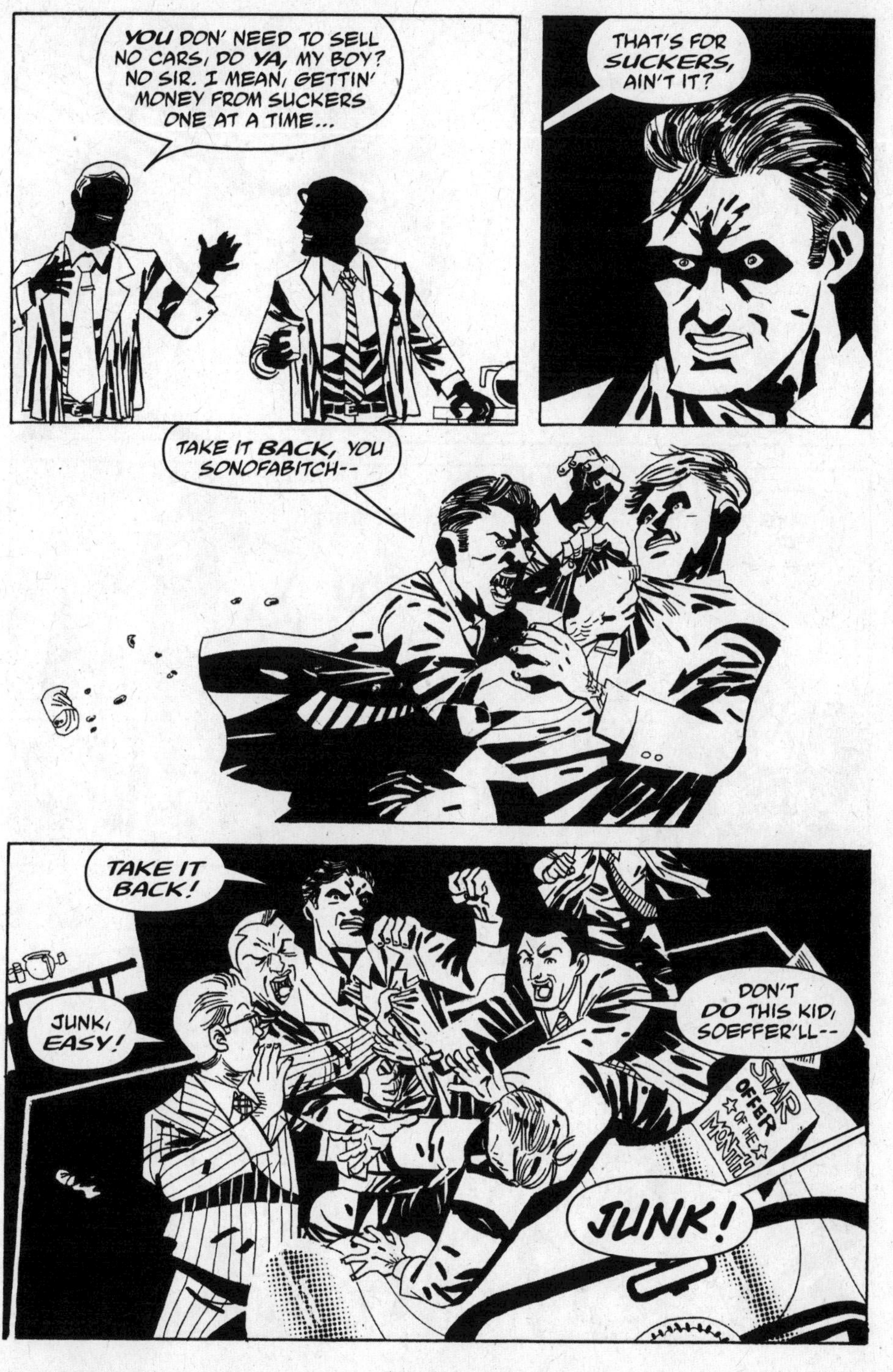
YOU DON' NEED TO SELL NO CARS, DO YA, MY BOY? NO SIR. I MEAN, GETTIN' MONEY FROM SUCKERS ONE AT A TIME...
THAT'S FOR SUCKERS, AIN'T IT?
TAKE IT BACK, YOU SONOFABITCH--
TAKE IT BACK!
JUNK, EASY!
DON'T DO THIS KID, SOEFFER'LL--
STAR OFFER OF THE MONTH
JUNK!

MY OFFICE.

NOW.

"TAKE IT BACK..."

NOT THE *FIRST* TIME WE HEARD THEM FUCKIN' WORDS TODAY, IS IT, FELLAS?

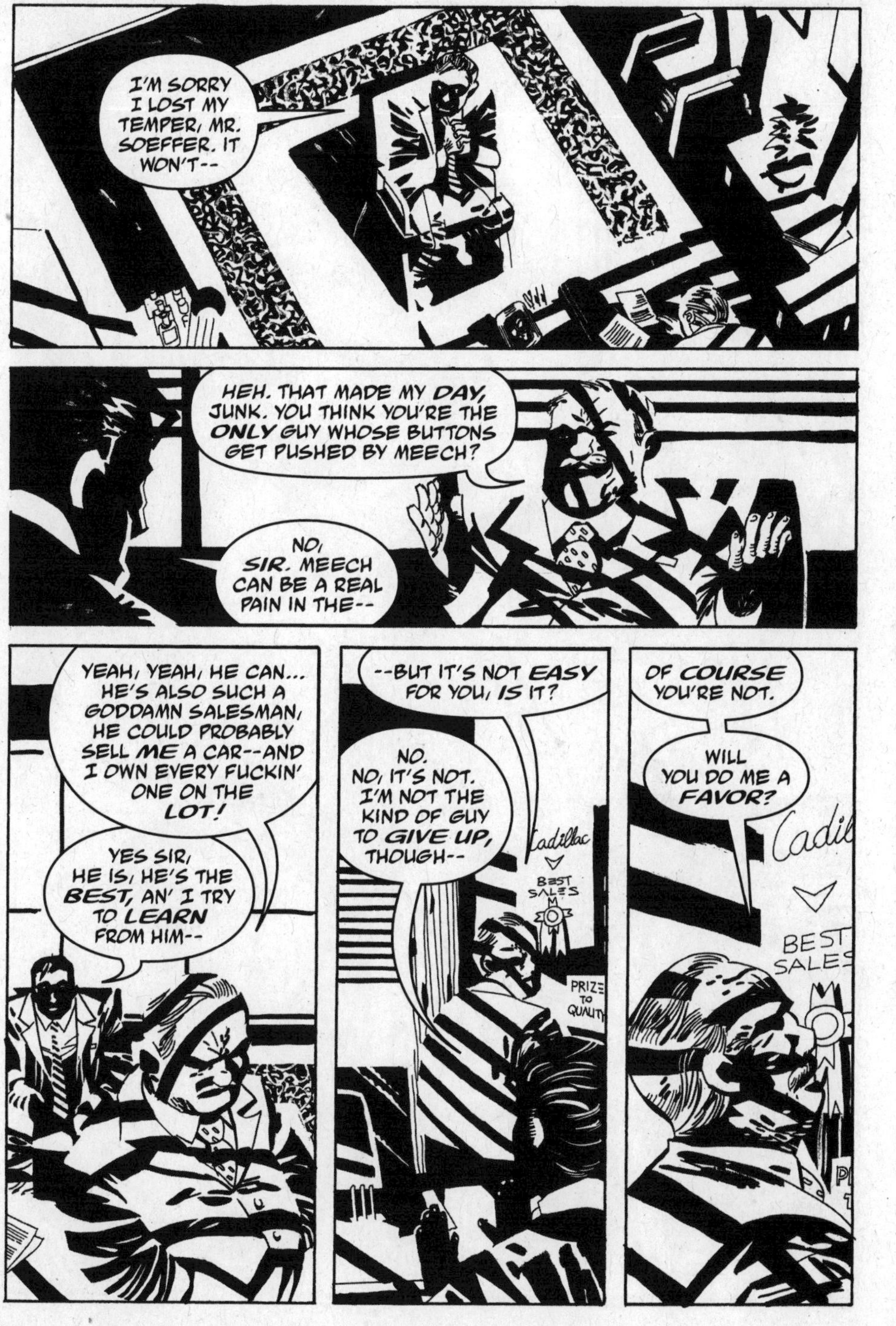
I'M SORRY I LOST MY TEMPER, MR. SOEFFER. IT WON'T--
HEH. THAT MADE MY DAY, JUNK. YOU THINK YOU'RE THE ONLY GUY WHOSE BUTTONS GET PUSHED BY MEECH?
NO, SIR. MEECH CAN BE A REAL PAIN IN THE--
YEAH, YEAH, HE CAN... HE'S ALSO SUCH A GODDAMN SALESMAN, HE COULD PROBABLY SELL ME A CAR--AND I OWN EVERY FUCKIN' ONE ON THE LOT!
YES SIR, HE IS, HE'S THE BEST, AN' I TRY TO LEARN FROM HIM--
--BUT IT'S NOT EASY FOR YOU, IS IT?
NO. NO, IT'S NOT. I'M NOT THE KIND OF GUY TO GIVE UP, THOUGH--
Cadillac
BEST SALES
PRIZE TO QUALITY
OF COURSE YOU'RE NOT.
WILL YOU DO ME A FAVOR?
BEST SALES

YES SIR, ANY--

STOP KISSING MY ASS.

IT'S A WASTE OF MY TIME...

AND YOURS.

YOU SOLD A CONVERTIBLE THE OTHER DAY...

YES. YES, SIR, I DID. IT WASN'T AN EASY SALE, NO LAY DOWN OR NOTHING, I CUT MY COMMISSION TO THE BONE--

--MEECH WOULD *NEVER* DO THAT. HE'D PUT THE GUY WHO COULD AFFORD A GALAXY--INTO A *GALAXY*, WITH EVERY BELL AND WHISTLE AVAILABLE, SO THE CUSTOMER WOULD DRIVE OFF THE LOT WITH WHAT HE BELIEVED WAS THE *BEST GALAXY ON THE ROAD...*

HE *WOULDN'T* STICK HIM IN A *FUCKING EL DORADO* THAT I HAD TO *TAKE BACK* TODAY! YOU HEARD ME RIGHT--WAS WITHIN *THE THREE-DAY GRACE!* WHAT DID I TELL YOU WAS THE *WORST DISEASE* A CUSTOMER COULD *EVER* GET?!

BUYER'S REMORSE.

BECAUSE IF A CUSTOMER FEELS HE WAS TAKEN *ADVANTAGE OF,* HE CAN RETURN THE CAR. AND HE'LL TELL--

DON'T FUCKING FEED ME MY OWN GODDAMN LINE!

YOU'RE A **SHIT** SALESMAN, JUNK. I KNEW THAT AFTER **ONE WEEK** OF YOU ON THE JOB.

BUT BEIN' SOMEWHAT OF A SPORTS STAR...YOU WERE GOOD FOR BUSINESS.

WERE?

YOU HEARD ME.

WHERE **YOU** GOING?

I JUST GOT **FIRED,** DIDN' I?

NO!... SIDDOWN. PLEASE.

YOU KNOW I HAVE A *DAUGHTER?*

YES, SIR. I'VE READ ABOUT HER.

THAT'S MY PROBLEM... *EVERYONE* HAS.

VICKI...SHE'S A *GOOD* GIRL, BUT...

...SHE MANAGES TO GET INTO A LOT OF TROUBLE. I CAN'T *HAVE* THAT. SOEFFER MOTORS IS THE LARGEST DEALERSHIP IN THE NORTHEAST. I'M ONE OF THE RICHEST MEN IN THE STATE.

I JUST CAN'T *HAVE* THAT.

YOU'RE A STRONG KID... GOOD WITH YOUR HANDS... INTIMIDATING WHEN YOU *WANT TO* BE...

VICKI **NEEDS** SOMEONE LIKE THAT AROUND HER. CAN YOU **BE** THAT FOR ME?

WHATEVER YOU NEED, SIR, I'M--

STOP KISSING MY ASS.

I CAN HANDLE YOUR PROBLEM, MR. SOEFFER.

WHEN I PROMISED SOEFFER I'D KEEP HIS DAUGHTER OUT OF TROUBLE, HE *LAUGHED* AT ME. THAT RUBBED THE *WRONG* WAY. "JUST KEEP HER OUT OF THE PAPERS," HE SAID.

HE WANTED IT DONE ON THE *Q.T.*, TOO-- VICKI WASN'T SUPPOSED TO KNOW ANYTHING ABOUT IT. I DIDN'T REALLY UNDERSTAND THAT, TOLD HIM THAT IT WOULD BE A LOT EASIER FOR ME IF I COULD BE *CLOSE* TO HER.

HE STARED AT ME THEN, AND SAID, "YOU DON'T KNOW HOW *WRONG* YOU ARE."

VICKI'S STOMPING GROUND WAS NEW YORK AFTER DARK--WHICH *ALSO* HAPPENED TO BE THE NAME OF ONE OF THE *GOSSIP COLUMNS* SHE FREQUENTED.

EVERY PAPER HAD ONE, THOUGH FOR THE LIFE OF ME, I DIDN'T KNOW WHY. THEY WERE A WASTE OF INK, AS FAR AS I WAS CONCERNED. I TRIED NOT TO EVER READ 'EM, THEY JUST PISSED ME OFF, FULL OF MADE-UP STORIES ABOUT PEOPLE I SHOULDN'T *CARE* ABOUT.

PEOPLE THAT DIDN'T HAVE A CARE IN THE *WORLD*.

PLENTY I RECOGNIZED, TOO. I MEAN, HOW *COULDN'T* I?--THEY ALWAYS HAD THEIR PICTURES IN THE PAPERS...

MARY AND ANNIE ASCOTT. THEY HAD A TELEVISION SHOW WHEN THEY WERE *KIDS,* "BRINGING UP THE TWINS," IT WAS CALLED. NOW?

THEY WERE FAMOUS FOR THE *MEN* WHO WALK IN AND OUT OF THEIR LIVES.

KATY DEE WAS FAMOUS TOO--BARELY TWENTY YEARS OLD, AN' ALREADY DIVORCED *TWICE.*

SHE WAS A SINGER, HAD A COUPLE OF HITS. I ADMIT "CRY FOR ME JOHNNY" WAS A CATCHY TUNE, BUT NOT REALLY MY KIND OF MUSIC.

NOT REALLY MY KIND OF *CROWD,* EITHER. STANDING IN THAT NIGHTCLUB, SURROUNDED, I WAS HAPPY AS A CLAM NOT TO BE ONE OF THESE PEOPLE. SURE, THEY HAD IT ALL, BUT THEY *FLAUNTED* IT. MAYBE NO ONE MORE THAN...

VICTORIA SOEFFER. DADDY'S LITTLE GIRL. HEIRESS TO THE LARGEST AUTOMOBILE DEALERSHIP ON THE EASTERN SEABOARD.

THAT ALONE MADE HER A *CELEBRITY...*

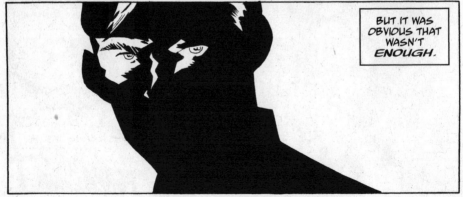

BUT IT WAS OBVIOUS THAT WASN'T *ENOUGH.*

OH KENNY-- YOU *SLAY* ME!

DO I? WELL, I'VE GOT SOMETHING YOU'D POSITIVELY *KILL* ME FOR...

HA HA HA HA HA HA HA HA

FRONT ROW CENTER TO WHAT'S SHAPING UP TO BE THE HOTTEST OPENING ON BROADWAY...

"LOVE'S LAST REQUITE." INTERESTED?

HHMPH. I WOULDN'T BE CAUGHT *DEAD* AT THAT SHOW...

HUH? WHAT GIVES? IT'S BEEN SOLD OUT FOR *MONTHS*...

THE ADVANCE REVIEWS ARE NOTHING SHORT OF STELLAR!

DEAR LITTLE BOY...

ONLY A *FOOL* BELIEVES EVERY-THING HE READS.

YEAH, VICKI WAS A REAL PIECE OF WORK ALL RIGHT. AND WHAT WITH THE WAY THE TRUST FUND JOES WERE BIRD-DOGGING HER, IT WASN'T ANY *WONDER* SHE GRABBED HEADLINES.

ALL THAT PLAY CAN MAKE A GIRL LOOK CHEAP--NO MATTER *HOW* LOADED SHE IS.

SHOULD A' *CHOKED UP* ON THE *BAT*, DIMAGGIO.

STOW IT, CLINT. THAT *BITCH*--I SHOULD CHOKE *HER!*

WELL, KENNETH-- YOU WOULDN'T BE THE *FIRST...*

THAT'S NO WAY TO SPEAK ABOUT A *LADY.*

WHO SAID ANYTHING *ABOUT ONE?*

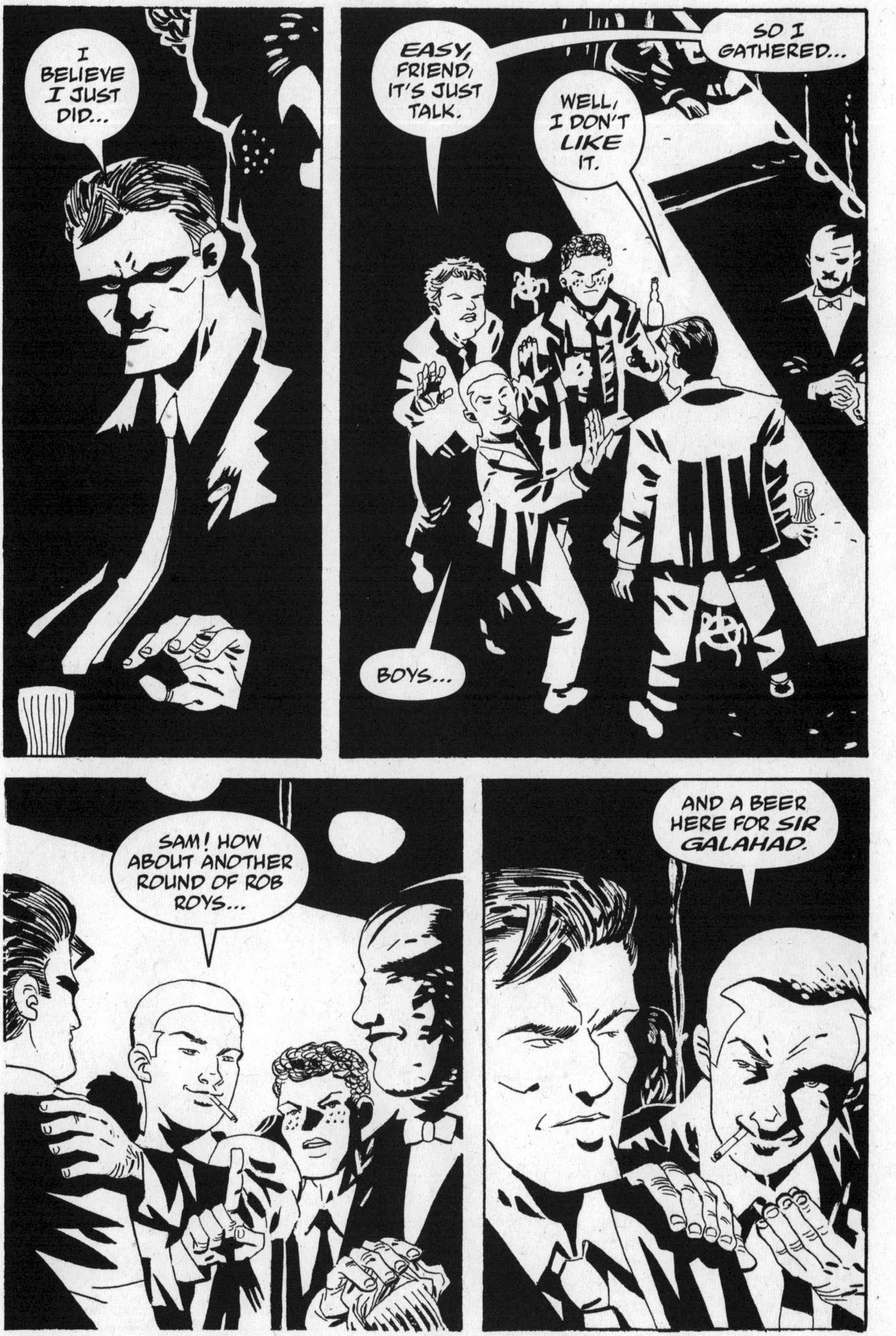
I BELIEVE I JUST DID...
EASY, FRIEND, IT'S JUST TALK.
SO I GATHERED...
WELL, I DON'T LIKE IT.
BOYS...
SAM! HOW ABOUT ANOTHER ROUND OF ROB ROYS...
AND A BEER HERE FOR SIR GALAHAD.

SO GALAHAD...

WHICH PRINCESS ARE YOU CHARGED WITH PROTECTING?

EXCUSE ME?

C'MON, LEVEL WITH ME, BUDDY. THAT SHINY *SUIT* DOESN'T HIDE WHAT'S OBVIOUSLY *UNDERNEATH*...

YOU ARE *MUSCLE*.

I DON'T KNOW WHAT YER *TALKIN'* ABOUT.

YES YOU DO, GALAHAD.

AND YOU CAN'T KEEP SECRETS FROM A *DRAGON*.

WEBSTER--

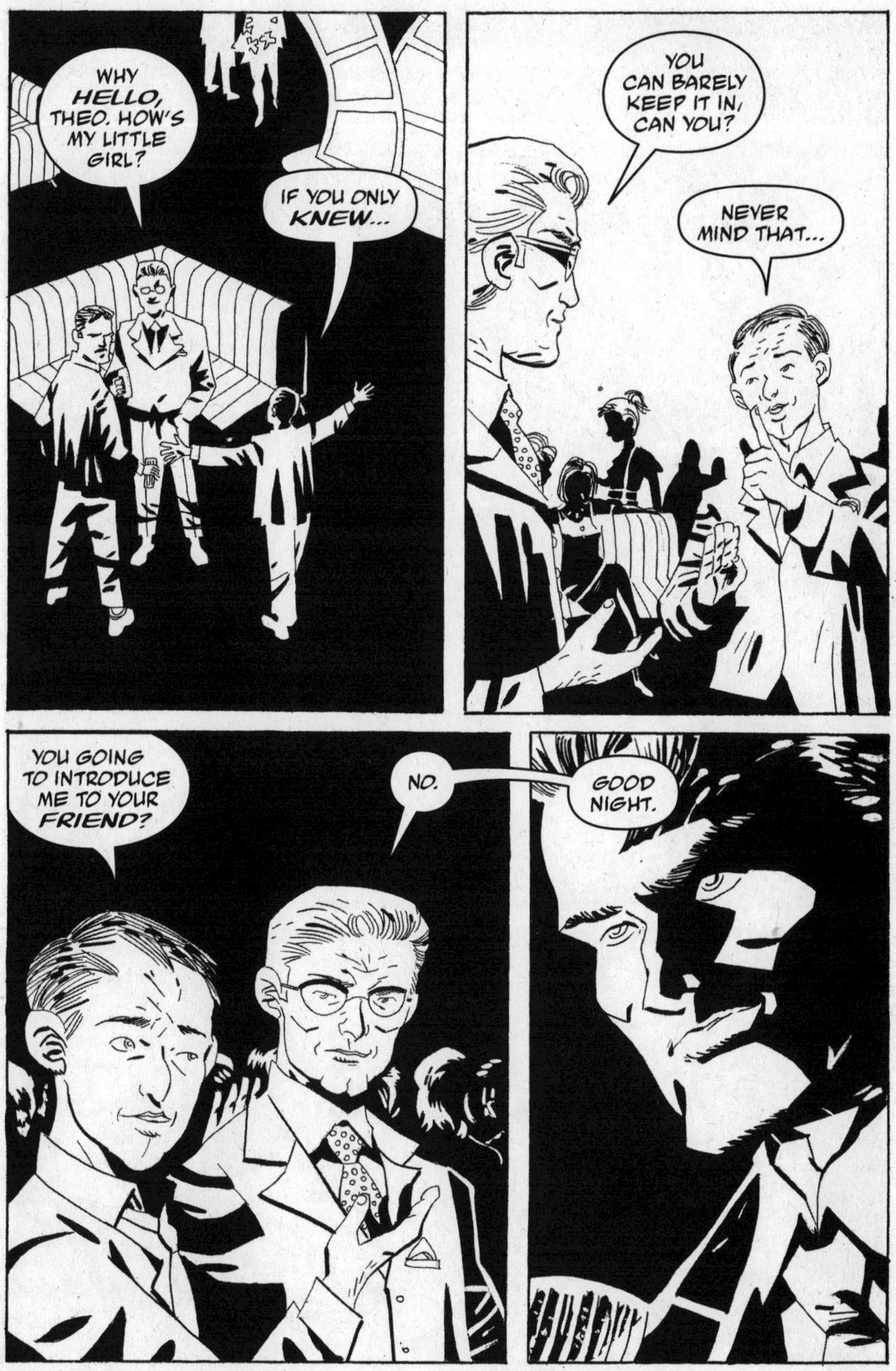
WHY HELLO, THEO. HOW'S MY LITTLE GIRL?
IF YOU ONLY KNEW...
YOU CAN BARELY KEEP IT IN, CAN YOU?
NEVER MIND THAT...
YOU GOING TO INTRODUCE ME TO YOUR FRIEND?
NO.
GOOD NIGHT.

VICKI DECIDED SHE WAS BORED ENOUGH AROUND MIDNIGHT, WHICH I THOUGHT WAS *EARLY*, CONSIDERING HER LATE-NIGHT REPUTATION.

NOT THAT I HAD A PROBLEM CALLING IT A NIGHT. WITH ALL THE FRENCH PERFUME AND UPPER WEST SIDE BULLSHIT IN THE CLUB, I NEEDED THE *FRESH AIR*.

THAT IS, UNTIL IT GOT A LITTLE *TOO* FRESH.

VICKI-- BABY--WAIT *UP*...

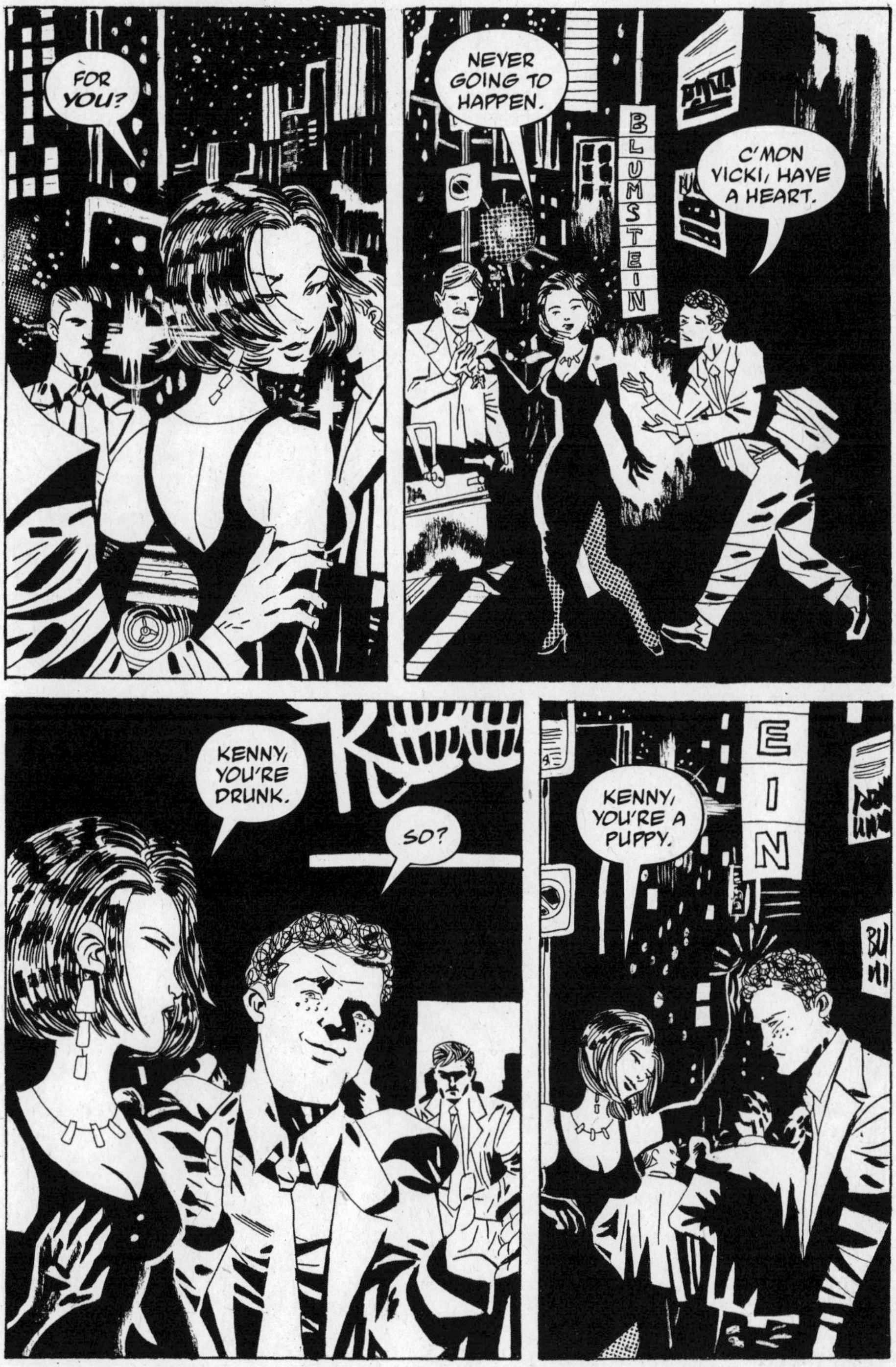
FOR YOU?
NEVER GOING TO HAPPEN.
BLUMSTEIN
C'MON VICKI, HAVE A HEART.
KENNY, YOU'RE DRUNK.
SO?
EIN
KENNY, YOU'RE A PUPPY.

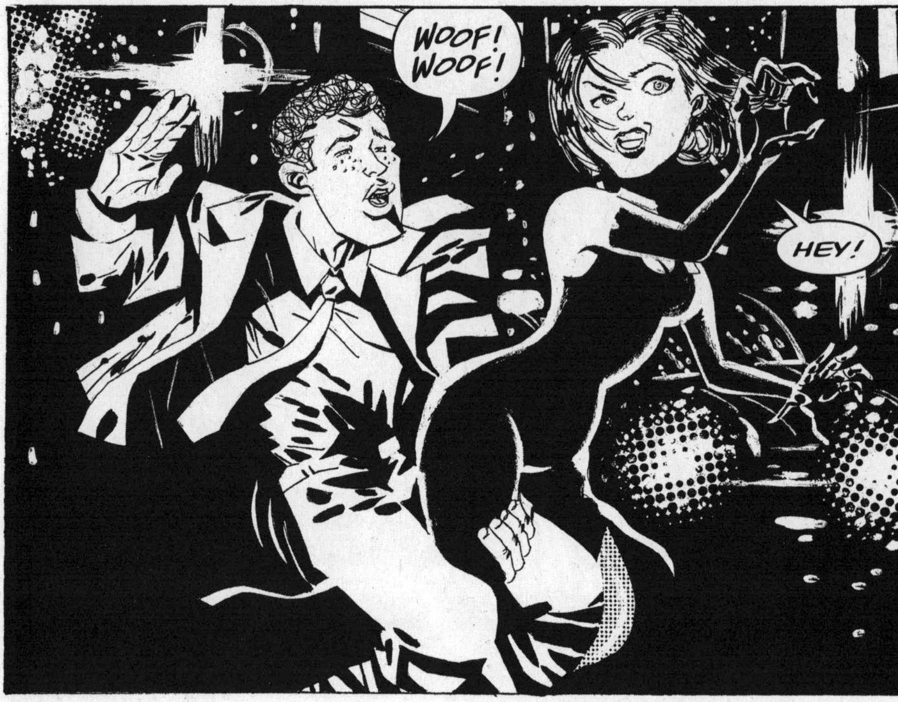
WOOF! WOOF!
HEY!

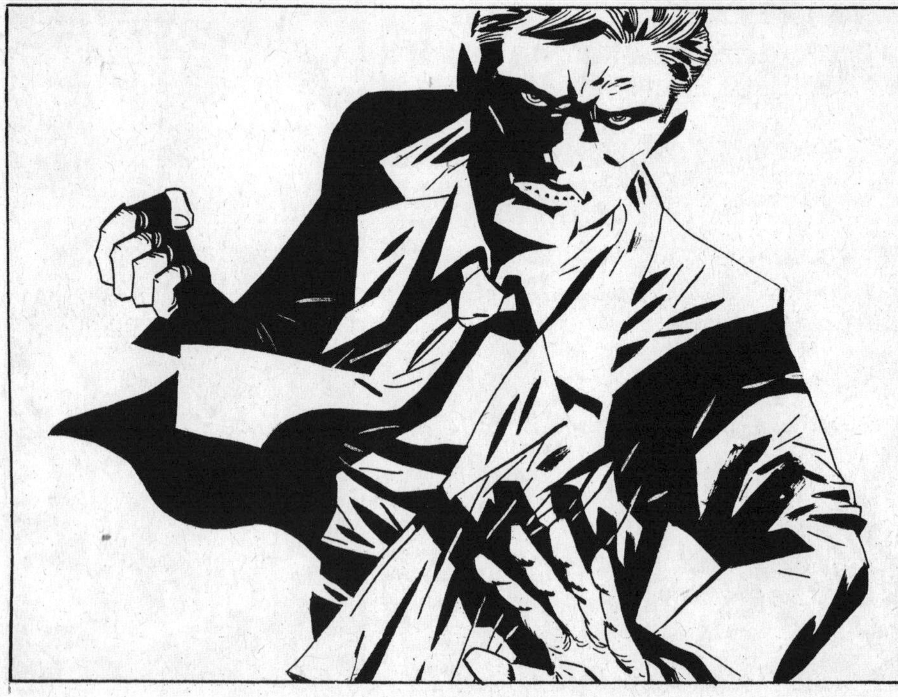

THAT'S **ENOUGH**, YOU SONOFABITCH!

POP

SMASH

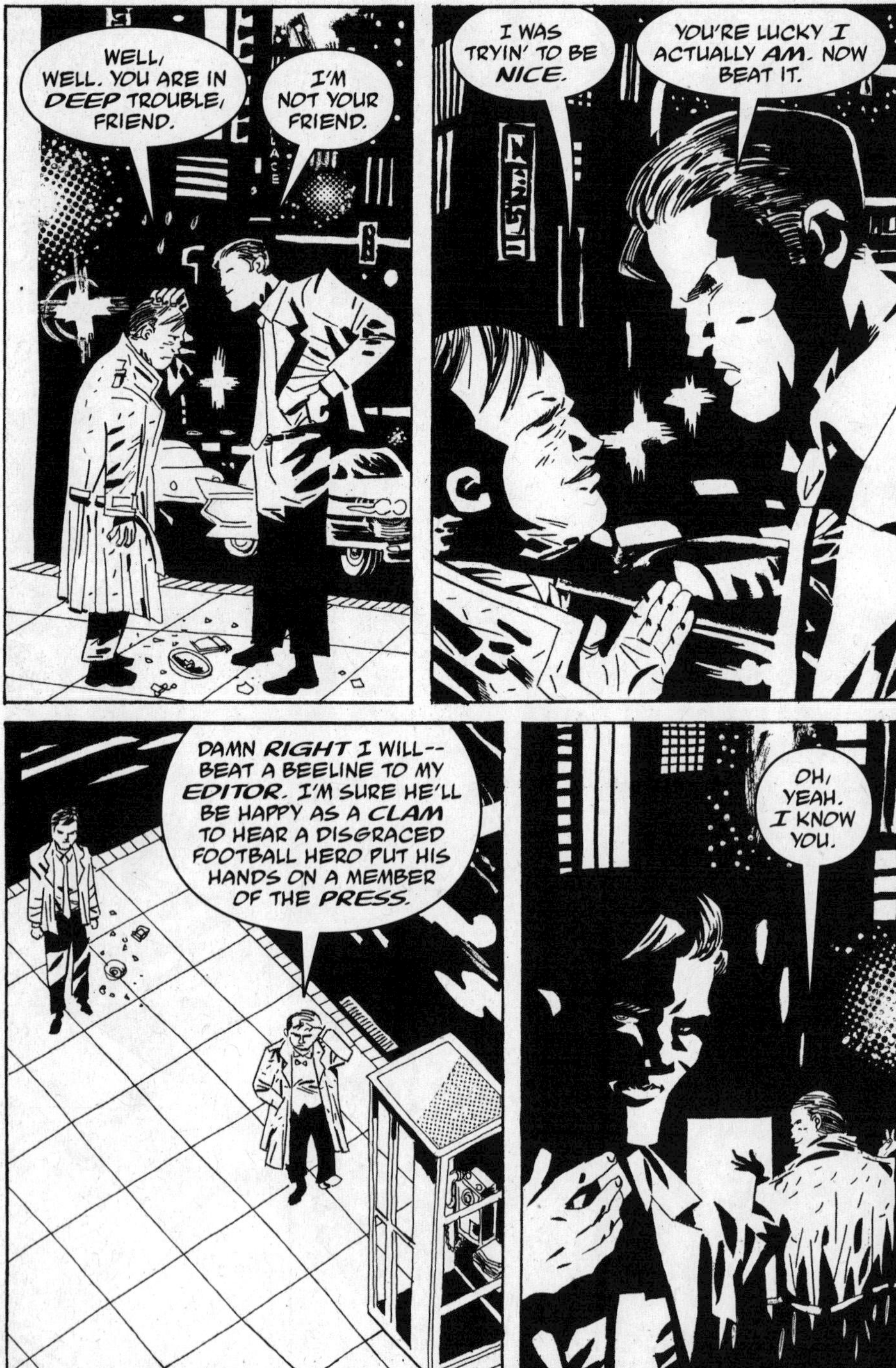
WELL, WELL. YOU ARE IN DEEP TROUBLE, FRIEND.
I'M NOT YOUR FRIEND.
I WAS TRYIN' TO BE NICE.
YOU'RE LUCKY I ACTUALLY AM. NOW BEAT IT.
DAMN RIGHT I WILL-- BEAT A BEELINE TO MY EDITOR. I'M SURE HE'LL BE HAPPY AS A CLAM TO HEAR A DISGRACED FOOTBALL HERO PUT HIS HANDS ON A MEMBER OF THE PRESS.
OH, YEAH. I KNOW YOU.

LOOK, I'M SORRY...

NOW YOU ARE. SORRY DON'T COVER MY LOSS, THOUGH.

BUT THEN, YOUR GAME AIN'T ABOUT COVERING.

MINE IS.

LUCKY YOU DO HAVE A FRIEND.

WHY'D YOU DO THAT?

WHAT? I OWE YOU ONE, PALLY. A PICTURE OF ME ABOUT TO HAVE MY ASS KICKED IS **NOT** SOMETHING I WANT TO SEE OVER TOAST AND BLOODY MARYS.

I'LL PAY YOU BACK, SOON AS I GET THE CHANCE.

I DOUBT YOU'LL **GET** ONE.

JAMES! WHERE TO NEXT?

THERE'S A REAL GONE COMBO RIPPIN' IT UP AT THE KIT KAT!

HARLEM IT IS THEN!

YOU COMING?

I FOLLOWED VICKI AND HER HIGH SOCIETY TRAIN UP TO THE NEXT CLUB, BUT I DECIDED TO STAY OUTSIDE.

I'D ALREADY GOTTEN TOO CLOSE FOR COMFORT--BOTH SOEFFFER'S AND MINE--AND I WASN'T ABOUT TO MAKE *THAT* MISTAKE AGAIN.

PLUS, I WASN'T IN THE BEST OF MOODS.

IT'S TRUE, THAT KENNY KID HAD BAILED ME OUT OF A REAL JAM, BUT HE DIDN'T HAVE TO BE SUCH A *PRICK* ABOUT IT.

OR MAYBE HE *DID*. ONE LOOK IN MY DIRECTION, WHY WOULD HE THINK I'M GOOD FOR IT? HELL, I WOULDN'T LOAN *MYSELF* FIVE BUCKS AND EXPECT TO SEE THE MONEY AGAIN.

THAT'S A SHITTY WAY TO *FEEL* ABOUT ONESELF...

SO I SWORE I'D PAY KENNY *BACK*.

EXCUSE ME...

51

CAN I TROUBLE YOU FOR A LIGHT?

MY NAME'S THEO.

NICE NIGHT, ISN'T IT?

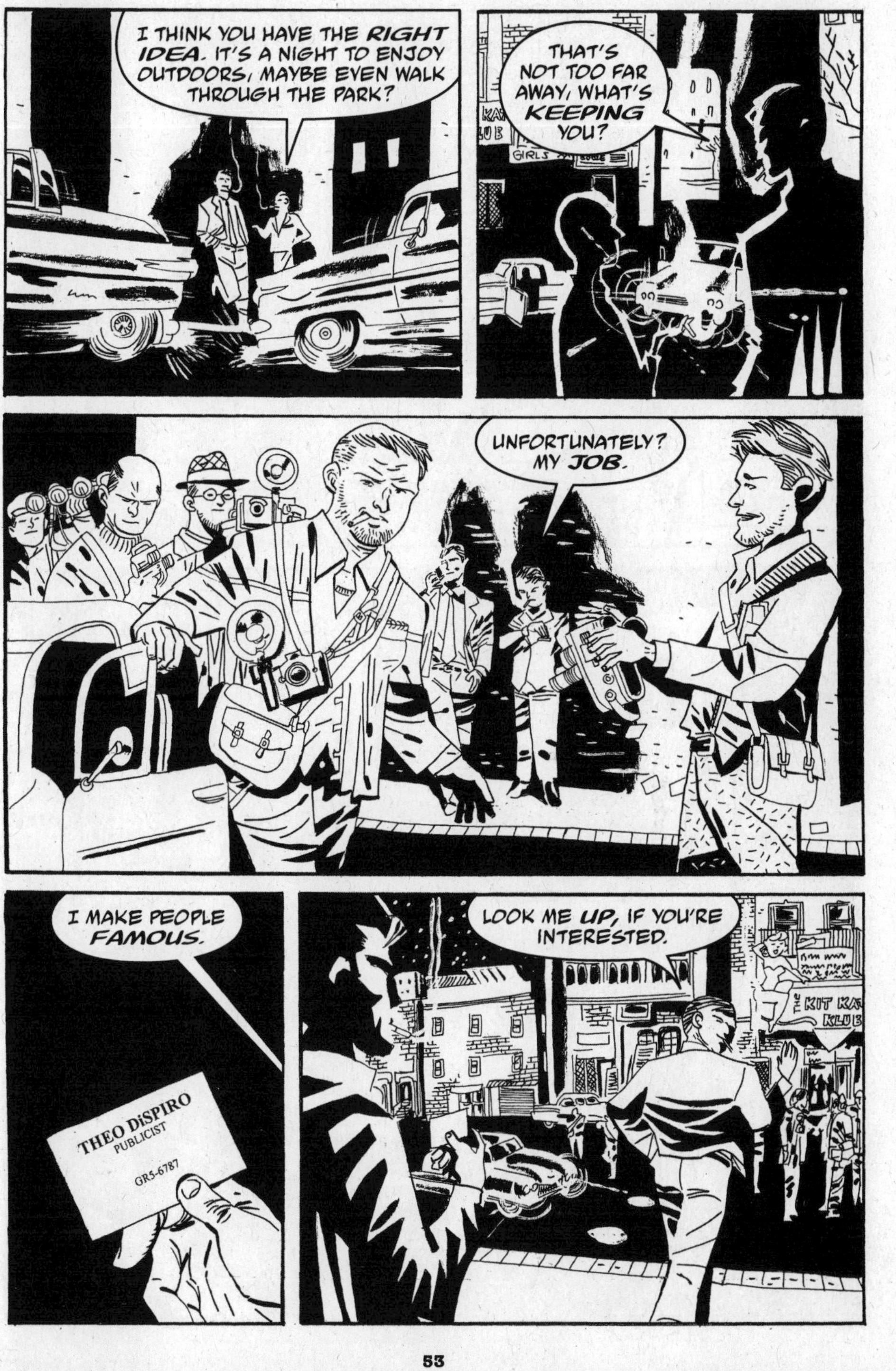
I THINK YOU HAVE THE *RIGHT IDEA*. IT'S A NIGHT TO ENJOY OUTDOORS, MAYBE EVEN WALK THROUGH THE PARK?
THAT'S NOT TOO FAR AWAY, WHAT'S *KEEPING* YOU?
GIRLS
UNFORTUNATELY? MY *JOB*.
I MAKE PEOPLE *FAMOUS*.
THEO DiSPIRO
PUBLICIST
GR5-6787
LOOK ME *UP*, IF YOU'RE INTERESTED.
THE KIT KA
KLUB

THAT MADE ME HOT... *REAL* HOT.

THE FUCKIN' *NERVE...*

THINKIN' I MIGHT BE INTERESTED IN WHAT *HE* HAD TO OFFER.

I WANTED TO DROP THAT LITTLE SONOFABITCH DOWN HARD ON THE PAVEMENT RIGHT *THEN...*

LET HIM KNOW EXACTLY WHAT IT *MEANT* TO BE FAMOUS.

BUT WHERE WOULD *THAT* GET ME?

NOT WHERE I **NEEDED** TO BE.

HEY PALLY! HAVE A DRINK...

JAMES HERE WAS JUST **TALKING** ABOUT YOU.

OH YEAH?

DOWN, BIG FELLA.

"I WAS JUST TELLING KENNY IT'S **UNWISE** TO PLAY THE FOOL AROUND AN **HONORABLE** MAN SUCH AS **YOURSELF.**"

WE'RE HIS FRIENDS, WE'RE ENTERTAINED BY HIS BAWDY BEHAVIOR, BUT NOT **EVERY-ONE** GETS THE JOKE.

YOU MEAN LIKE *THAT* GUY.

WHO?

"THAT RUNT BY THE DOOR. YOU *KNOW* HIM?"

NEVER *SEEN* HIM BEFORE.

KITCHEN

WELL *HE* KNOWS *YOU.* COMING IN I OVERHEARD HIM SAY TO THAT CHICK HE'S MAKIN' THAT KENNY WASN'T FUNNY--THAT KENNY WAS A FUCKIN' *JOKE,* AN' HE WAS GONNA *SHOW* HIM...

...SOON AS HE GOT THE *CHANCE.*

WHEN I PLAYED THE GAME, MY COACHES WERE ALWAYS CHEWIN' ME OUT FOR BEING *OUT OF POSITION.*

THEY'D GET RED IN THE FACE AND *SPIT* IN *MINE* FOR NOT FOLLOWING THE *GAME PLAN.*

EVEN WHEN *I* KNEW IT WASN'T *WORKING.*

THEY NEVER COULD GET IT THROUGH THEIR FAT HEADS THAT THE GAME ON THE *FIELD* WAS NOT THE ONE THEY WANTED IT TO BE ON THE *SIDELINES.*

THEY'D FUCK ME A NEW ASSHOLE, THEN HAND ME THE GAME BALL FOR *WINNING* IT FOR THEM.

I NEVER TRUSTED THEM. I WAS *IN* THE GAME. AND I WASN'T NEVER THE KIND OF PLAYER THAT LET THE GAME COME *TO* HIM...

I HAD TO GET *CLOSE.*

LET'S GO...

SURE.

WHERE ARE WE GOING?

WHERE *WERE* WE GOING? *HELL* IF I *KNEW*--AND IF I ONLY KNEW THEN...

...HOW **RIGHT** I WAS.

SO...

YOU MY **NEW** MAN?

?

WHAT? THOUGHT YOU'D BE MY **FIRST**?

HARDLY.

≋SIGH≋...NO, THERE'S BEEN A **STRING** OF MEN MY FATHER HAS HIRED TO KEEP THEIR EYES ON ME.

HIRED 'EM, AND FIRED 'EM, JUST LIKE THAT.

DO YOU HAVE A NAME?

MY FRIENDS CALL ME *JUNK*.

WHAT'S YOUR *NAME*?

RICH.

RICH...

PLEASE DON'T TAKE ME HOME.

YOU GOT NOWHERE ELSE TO *GO*, MISS SOEFFER.

MY FRIENDS CALL ME *VICKI*.

LOOK VICKI, IT'S LATE. I'M SURE YOUR FATHER--

--*NO* YOU'RE NOT. YOU HAVEN'T A *CLUE* TO WHAT HE'S THINKING.

HE WORRIES ABOUT HIS LITTLE *GIRL.*

IS *THAT* WHAT HE TOLD YOU? *LOOK* AT ME, RICH...

DO *YOU* SEE A LITTLE GIRL?

SHAME ON YOU, RICH...

MAYBE YOU *DO* KNOW WHAT DADDY'S THINKING.

YOU BETTER LET ME OUT *HERE*...

YOU'RE SUPPOSED TO STAY *AWAY* FROM ME, RIGHT?

DON'T WORRY, YOUR INDISCRETION'S *SAFE* WITH ME.

I'LL TELL HIM I HAD THE CAB DRIVER DROP ME OFF ON THE ROAD, SO AS NOT TO EMBARRASS HIM.

MAYBE I WON'T EVEN *MENTION* THAT I MADE A NEW FRIEND...

AS I WATCHED VICKI WALK UP THE DRIVEWAY, I SWEAR I HEARD HER OLD MAN *LAUGHING* AGAIN...

LIKE HE'D GIVEN ME *ANOTHER* JOB I WAS NO GOOD AT.

OR MAYBE IT *WASN'T* HIM. MAYBE IT WAS HIS LITTLE *GIRL* WHO LAUGHED...

DARING ME TO BE *GOOD.*

WHEN SHE DISAPPEARED, I DROVE AROUND FOR A WHILE. THERE WAS A LOT ON MY MIND, AND I COULDN'T *SLEEP...*

SO I WOKE SOMEBODY ELSE UP.

I WAS ANGRY, BUT IT WAS *GOOD*...

IT WAS *ANGRY*.

MMM, BABY... DIDN'T EXPECT TO FEEL YOU 'TIL *MONDAY.*

MONDAY?

...OH YEAH, THE SHORE. *ABOUT* THAT, CHARLENE...

YOU CAN'T *MAKE* IT? *THAT* WHY YOU CAME BY TONIGHT?

NO...AND NO, IT'S *NOT* WHY.

I GOT A NEW JOB...

RICH, WHAT *HAPPENED*-- WHY DIDN'T YOU *TELL* ME?

I *AM* TELLING YOU!

LOOK CHARLENE, THE *CAR* THING? I WASN'T KIDDIN' *ANYBODY*-- LEAST OF ALL THE *BOSS*.

SO...I'M WORKING *SECURITY* FOR HIM NOW.

IT'S GONNA BE EVERY NIGHT FER A WHILE, 'TIL I GET THE HANG OF IT.

I'M SORRY.

WHY...

BECAUSE WE GET TO SPEND OUR *DAYS* TOGETHER?

SHE HUGGED ME. I SMILED.

AND THEN I WAS ANGRY ALL *OVER* AGAIN.

I DIDN'T GET MUCH SLEEP THE NEXT FEW WEEKS. MY NIGHTS WERE SPENT IN CLUBS, KEEPING PEOPLE I DIDN'T LIKE AWAY FROM VICKI. AND MY *DAYS*...

IN BED. I KNEW CHARLENE MIGHT HAVE WANTED TO GO OUT-- LUNCH, OR TO THE PARK, WINDOW SHOPPING. WALKING, ARM IN ARM...

...BUT I JUST COULDN'T DEAL WITH IT. I DIDN'T WANT TO BE AROUND ANYBODY.

AFTER THE *NIGHTS*, I JUST *NEEDED*...

VICKI MAY HAVE KEPT OUR RELATIONSHIP A SECRET FROM HER FATHER, BUT AS FOR HER *FRIENDS?*

SHE INTRODUCED ME AS HER *BODYGUARD.* IT DIDN'T TAKE LONG FOR WHO I WAS TO MAKE THE ROUNDS.

SO JUNK, THE GIANTS ARE GIVING SIX AND A HALF ON SUNDAY...

DON' GET ME WRONG, JAMES-- GIANTS GONNA *WIN* THAT GAME-- BUT ON FIELD GOALS. THE HALF POINT IS FOR SUCKERS ONLY.

THANKS, OL' KID. YOU'RE *TOPS* IN MY BOOK.

TAKIN' THE *POINTS,* I WERE YOU. LIONS' DEE, IT'S STINGY WITH THE END ZONE.

MY, AREN'T *YOU* THE GREAT SAGE...

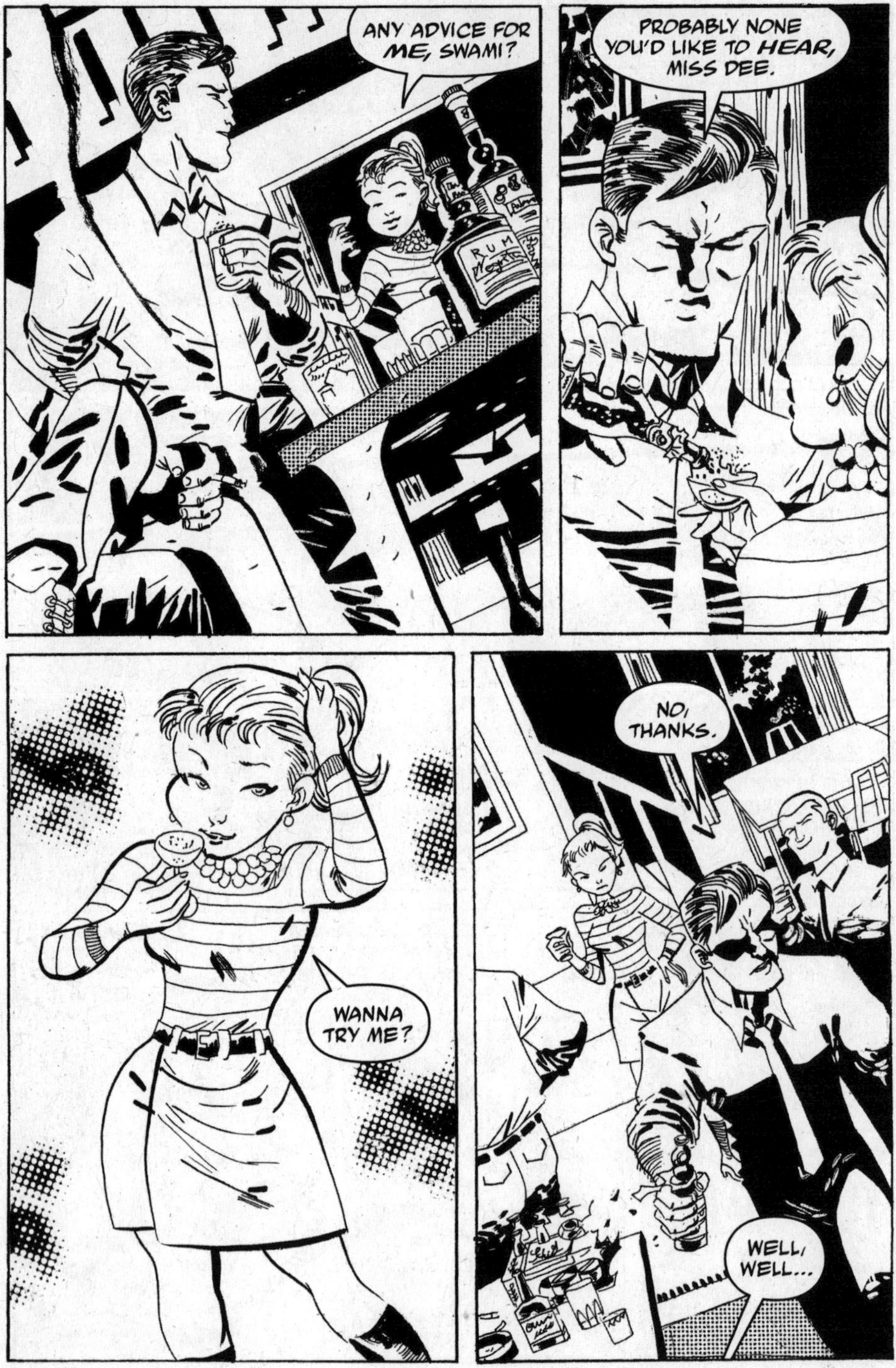
ANY ADVICE FOR ME, SWAMI?
PROBABLY NONE YOU'D LIKE TO HEAR, MISS DEE.
WANNA TRY ME?
NO, THANKS.
WELL, WELL...

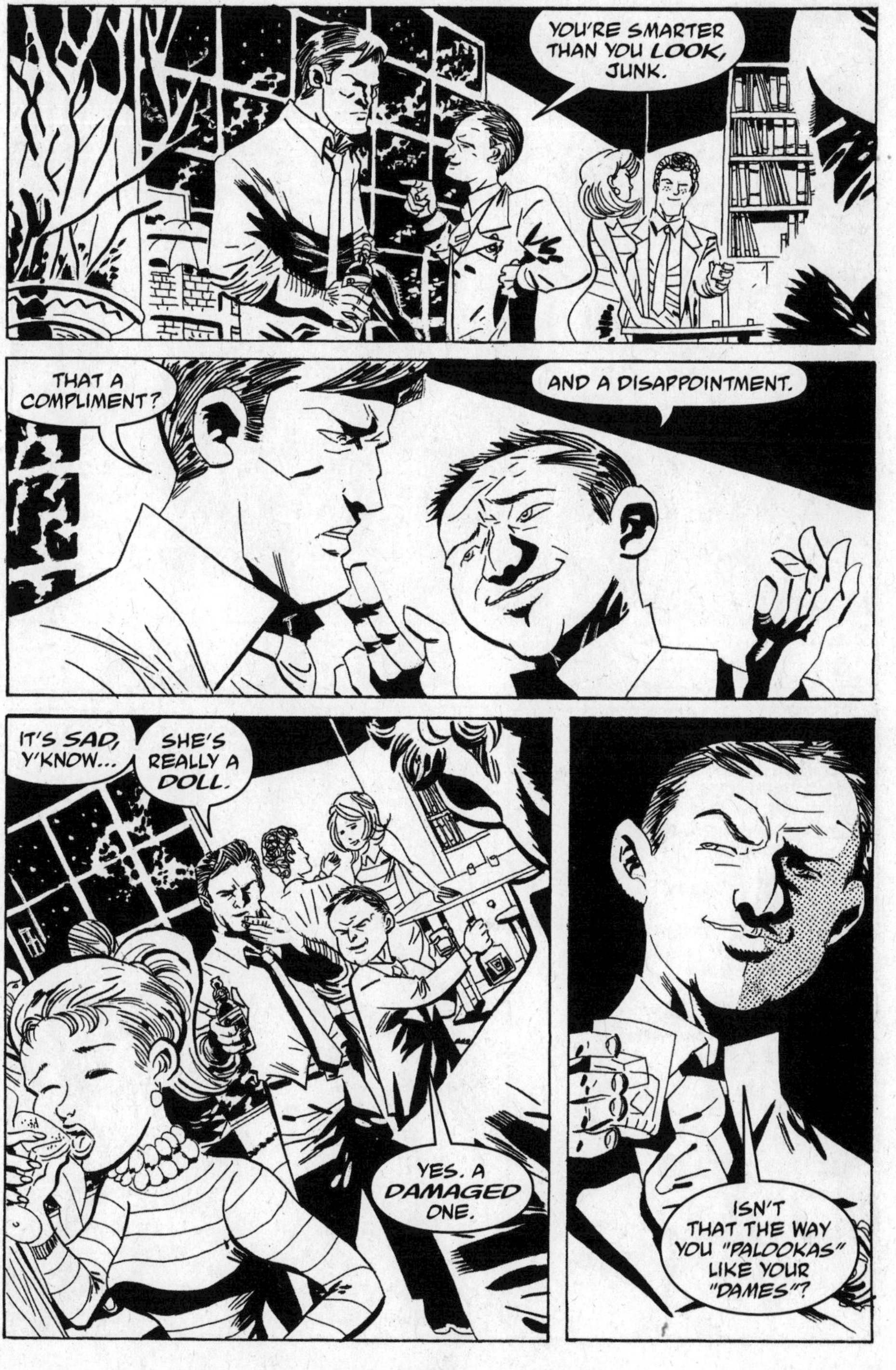
YOU'RE SMARTER THAN YOU LOOK, JUNK.
THAT A COMPLIMENT?
AND A DISAPPOINTMENT.
IT'S SAD, Y'KNOW...
SHE'S REALLY A DOLL.
YES. A DAMAGED ONE.
ISN'T THAT THE WAY YOU "PALOOKAS" LIKE YOUR "DAMES"?

FUCK YOU, THEO.

THAT'S BETTER. WE ALMOST SHARED A MOMENT, YOU AND I.

FAT CHANCE A' THAT.

JUNK, *PLEASE.* JUST BECAUSE WE FIND OUR *JOBS* AT CROSS PURPOSES, DOESN'T MEAN WE HAVE TO BE CROSS WITH EACH *OTHER.*

I MEAN, WHEN YOU WERE A *SPORTS STAR,* DIDN'T YOU HAVE FRIENDS WHO PLAYED FOR THE *OTHER TEAM?*

HEY, PALLY!

GOT MY **MONEY?**

JUS' **KIDDIN'**, JUS' **KIDDIN'**. LISTEN, ME AN' A FEW A' THE GANG, WE'RE GOING OUT TO THE **BOATHOUSE**, DO A LITTLE **DANCIN'**. INTERESTED?

NAH, I'M NOT MUCH OF A **DANCER**.

JEES...

I'M TALKIN' ABOUT **TWISTIN' THE NIGHT AWAY**.

I'M NOT MUCH FOR **THAT**, EITHER.

SO IT'S NOT JUST YOUR **JAW** THAT'S **SQUARE**...

HA HA.

WHAT ABOUT *YOU*, VICKI? CARE FOR A LITTLE ROLL IN THE GRASS?

WHY, *KENNY*...SUCH *CHEEK*...

AND RIGHT IN FRONT OF MY *CHAPERONE*, NO LESS.

AW, IT'S *COOL* WITH JUNK--AIN'T THAT *RIGHT*, BIG GUY?

WHAT IF I SAY *NO*?

WHAT IF...

...NOBODY LISTENS?   ...

HEY, DOLL, NO NEED TO MAKE THE PARTY *HOSTILE*...WE'RE *FRIENDS* HERE.

HOW ABOUT *I'M* THE ONE THAT SAYS NO THEN, AND WE'RE *ALL* OFF THE HOOK?

DO WHAT YOU WANNA DO, VICKI...

AND I'LL JUST DO MY JOB.

SPOKEN LIKE THE TRUE SALT OF THE EARTH!

...

HEY... ISN'T THAT--

SALLY-- HOW HAVE YOU BEEN, DEAR!?

SALLY PETRI. UNLIKE MOST OF THE PEOPLE I'D MET RECENTLY, SHE WAS FAMOUS FOR ALL THE *RIGHT* REASONS--

TALENT.

I'D SEEN MOST OF HER PICTURES-- "THE BORED AND THE BRAVE," "WALK WITH ANGER," "FINNEGAN'S DAUGHTERS"...

SHE WAS THE REAL DEAL--NOT SOME SPOILED KID TRADING HEADLINES ON A TRUST FUND. SHE WAS WHAT EVERYBODY ELSE *WANTED* TO BE...

SALLY WAS A *STAR*...

SO WHAT IF I GOT MOON-EYED?

77

I MEAN REALLY, SO *WHAT?*

MMPHH.

DID SOMEBODY OPEN A *WINDOW* IN HERE? IT SEEMS TO HAVE GOTTEN A BIT *CHILLY...*

VICKI!

SALLY-- *DARLING!*

NO ONE TOLD ME *YOU'D* BE HERE...

YOU ARE GETTING *RAVES* FOR "LOVE'S LAST REQUITE"-- JUST *RAVES!*

IT MUST FEEL WONDERFUL TO SHUT UP ALL THOSE NASTY CRITICS WHO SAID YOUR "TALENTS" WERE BUILT FOR THE *SCREEN* AND NOT THE *STAGE.*

WELL, ACTING IS ACTING. IT *IS* HARDER TO DO IN FRONT OF A LIVE AUDIENCE...

DON'T *SHE* KNOW IT...

COME, SIT DOWN... WE'VE GOT SO MUCH TO CATCH UP ON...

JUNK, BE A GOOD BOY, GET MISS PETRI A DRINK?

FRESHEN ME UP TOO, DEAR.

JUST YOUR JOB...EH, PALLY?

BEST HOP *TO* IT.

VICKI HAD ME *STINGING.* SHE'D CUT ME DOWN JUST TO MAKE HERSELF LOOK BETTER, AND I DIDN'T *DESERVE* THAT.

LOOKING BACK, I SHOULD HAVE LET IT ROLL OFF MINE. IF I HAD, MAYBE THINGS WOULD HAVE TURNED OUT *DIFFERENT.*

OR MAYBE *NOT.*

SHE TRIED TO HIDE IT, BUT SALLY WAS THE TYPE OF WOMAN WHO ROCKED VICKI'S OTHERWISE UNSHAKABLE CONFIDENCE.

SHE NEEDED TO IMPRESS SALLY.

SO TO GET BACK AT HER, I FIGURED NO HARM DOING THE *SAME.*

HERE YOU GO, MISS SOEFFER...

I'M SORRY, MISS PETRI--

CALL ME *SALLY.*

--SALLY, I DIDN'T ASK YOU WHAT YOU'D LIKE TO DRINK.

VODKA GIMLET.

A VODKA GIMLET?... I DON'T REALLY KNOW HOW TO *MAKE* ONE OF THOSE...

IT'S EASY.

CAN YOU SHOW ME?

82

SO...?

NOT BAD FOR A *BEGINNER.*

I'M A QUICK STUDY.

AND I CATCH ON FAST.

VICKI TELLS ME YOU PLAYED FOOTBALL... MISTER *JUNKIN,* IS IT?

RICH--OR *JUNK.* THAT'S WHAT I GO BY.

I PREFER *RICH...*

THOUGH YOU SEEM MORE COMFORTABLE WITH *JUNK.*

SO TELL ME, HOW DOES ONE GO FROM STIFF ARMING TO **STRONG** ARMING?

A CHEAP SHOT.

I DIDN'T MEAN TO--

--MY **KNEE.** PRAYERS AND BUBBLEGUM ARE ALL THAT'S HOLDING IT TOGETHER.

OH. I'M SORRY TO **HEAR** THAT.

WHY?

WELL, I LIKE THIS SONG, AND I WAS ABOUT TO ASK YOU TO DANCE...

AM I BEING TOO FORWARD?

DO YOU MIND IF I **LEAD?**

I NEVER MENTIONED THIS, NOT TO *ANY-BODY*, BECAUSE, WELL...

IT WAS NOBODY'S FUCKIN' BUSINESS, BUT MOST OF THE TIME?

MY KNEE...IT HURT. *CONSTANTLY*, REMINDING ME...

...ABOUT ME. I *HATED* IT, MY KNEE, BECAUSE IT WOULDN'T LET ME FORGET. BUT WHILE I WAS DANCING WITH SALLY, AS ONE SONG PLAYED INTO THE NEXT...

...I FORGOT ABOUT *IT*, ME...

...AND VICKI.

TEARS ON YOUR PILLOW, TO-- NIGH--HI-HI-HI-- HIGHT!

I'M READY FOR A BREATHER IF YOU DON'T MIND, JUNK.

NO, NO, NOT AT *ALL.* I'LL FETCH US ANOTHER ROUND OF REFRESHMENTS, OKAY?

WONDERFUL.

I AM, *AREN'T* I?

YES SIR, I CERTAINLY WAS. I LOOKED AROUND TO SEE WHAT KIND OF *REVIEW* MY LITTLE SHOW WAS GETTING.

IT WASN'T UNTIL THEN I NOTICED MY AUDIENCE HAD *WALKED OUT.*

THERE WERE TWENTY-THREE ROOMS IN THAT HOUSE, I LOOKED IN EACH ONE TWICE, THEN ONCE MORE...

NO VICKI.

SHE'D DISAPPEARED. PROBABLY JUST TO PISS ME OFF, OR WORSE-- GET ME IN TROUBLE WITH HER OLD MAN.

UP 'TIL THEN, I'D KEPT HER OUT OF THE PAPERS.

I WAS PRETTY SURE *THAT'S* WHERE SHE WANDERED OFF TO.

I FELT LIKE SOME FUCKIN' WALK-ON ROOKIE, MY HEAD UP MY ASS BECAUSE THAT'S THE PLACE IT WAS *MEANT* TO BE.

SO I WENT OUTSIDE, TO GET SOME AIR, AND COME UP WITH AN EXCUSE THAT WOULD FLY WITH SOEFFER. *THAT'S* WHEN I REALIZED...

EVERYONE ELSE WAS STILL AT THE *PARTY.*

NO, NOT *EVERY-ONE*...

THA'CHOO, GALAHAD?...

NO... PLEASE... STOP...

?

NO...

VICKI... BABY...

SO BEAUTIFUL... PLEASE...

THE AIR SMELLED SWEET. I COULDN'T BREATHE.

I'D READ STORIES IN THE PAPERS, ABOUT GUYS WHO'D SNAPPED...

WHO DID THINGS--
AWFUL THINGS--
THEY SAID THEY
DIDN'T REMEMBER.

AND *I* ALWAYS
CALLED IT
BULLSHIT.

A PLACE
I WAS
ALL TOO
FAMILIAR
WITH.

I FIGURED I WAS READING
ABOUT FELLAS WHO JUST
GOT PUSHED SO HARD TO
PLACES THEY NEVER
BELIEVED THEY COULD
GO, IT MADE THEM *HATE*
THEMSELVES.

BUT I WAS
WRONG.

I DIDN'T HATE MYSELF AS I FELT KENNY'S SMARMY FACE TURN TO HAMBURGER.

AND WHEN HE STOPPED BREATHING, I **STARTED** TO AGAIN.

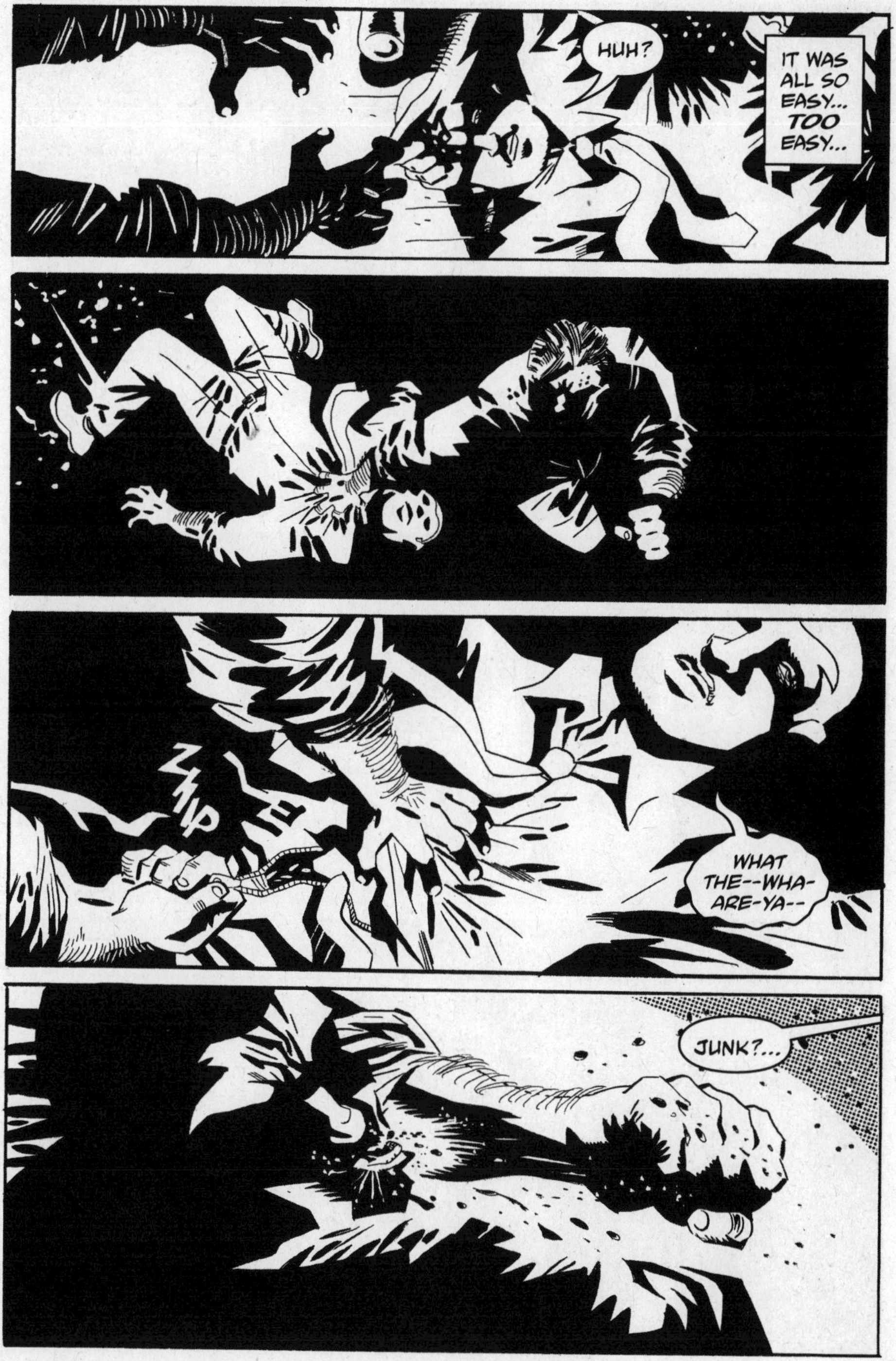
HUH?
IT WAS ALL SO EASY... TOO EASY...
ZZIP
WHAT THE--WHA-ARE-YA--
JUNK?...

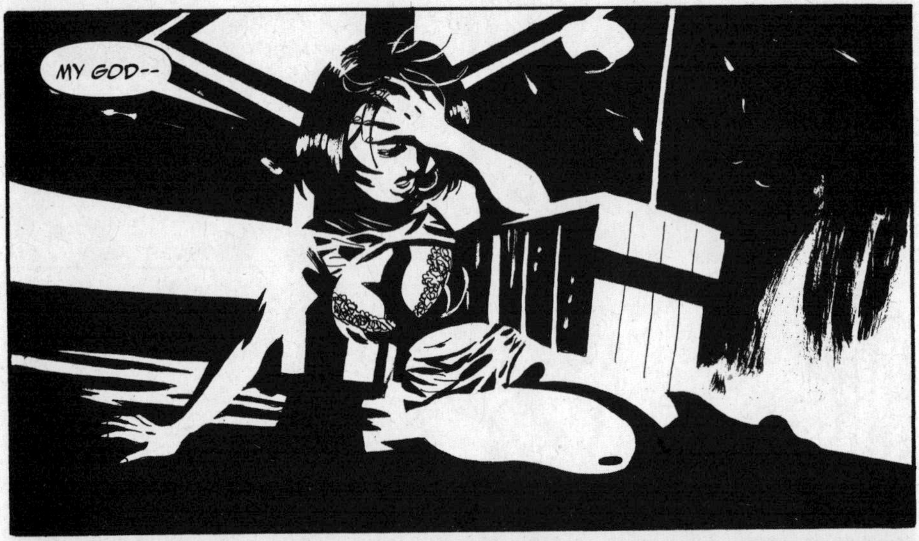
MY GOD--

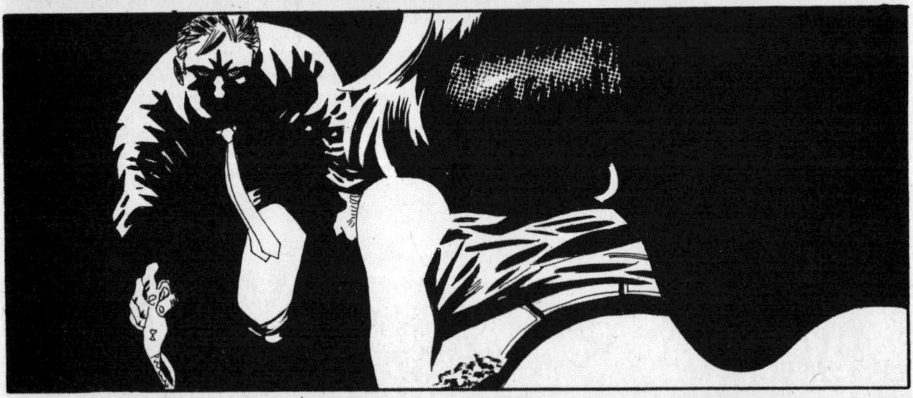

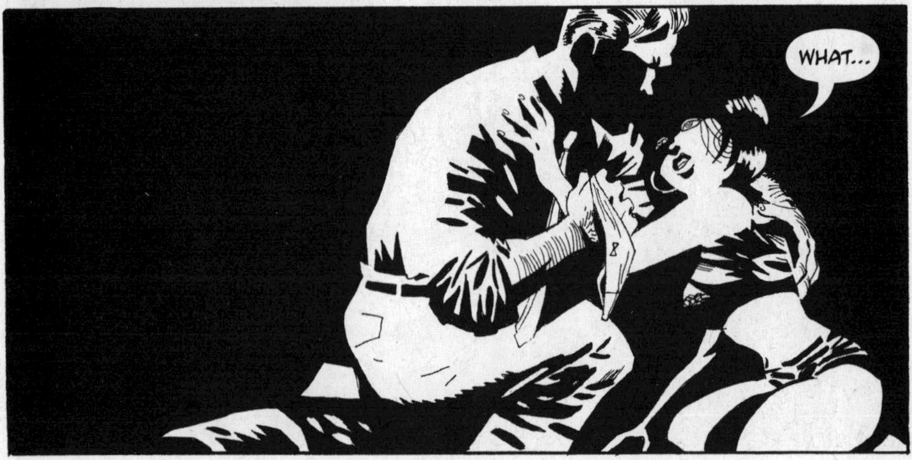
WHAT...

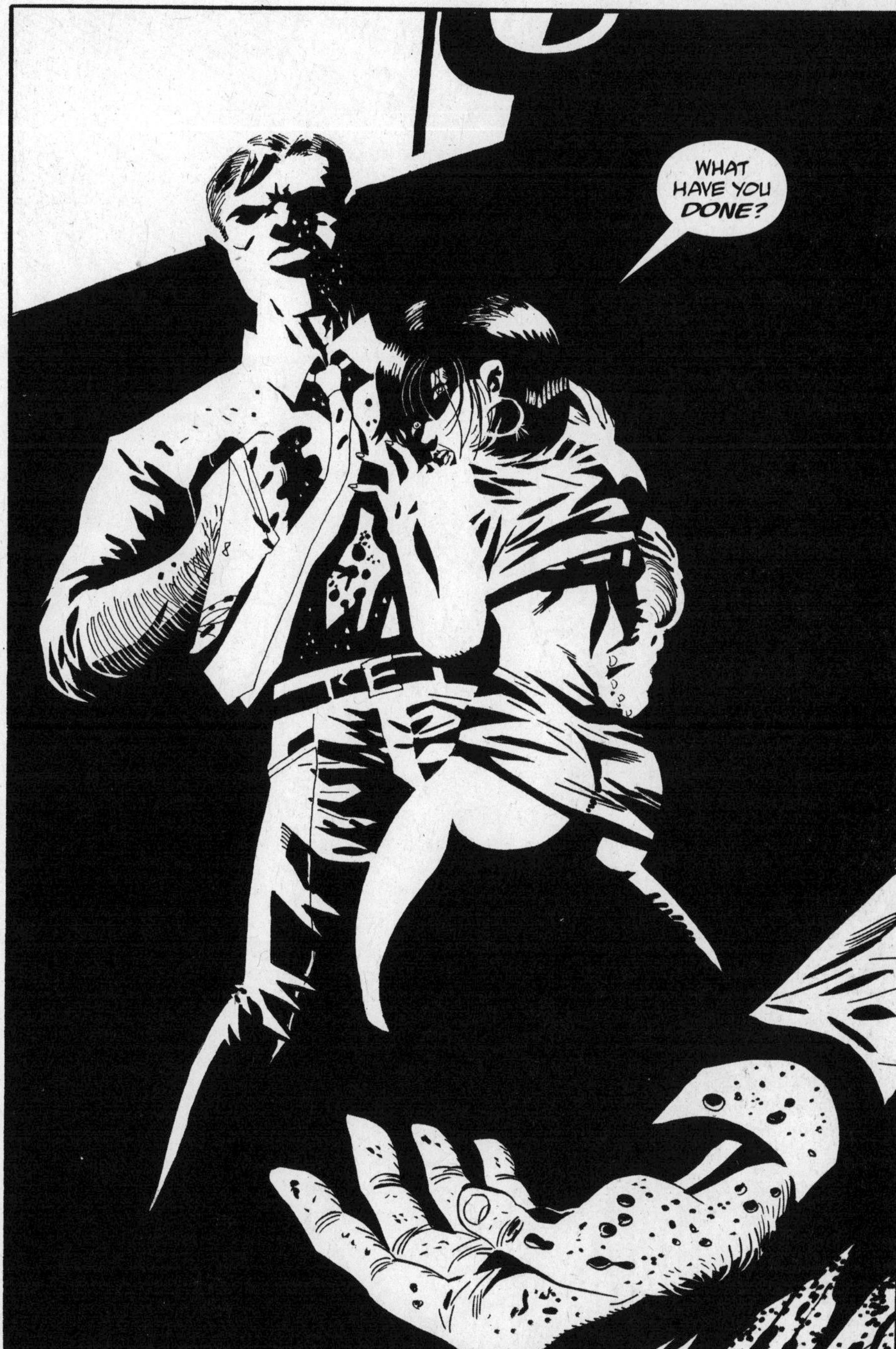
WHAT HAVE YOU DONE?

YOU PUNK.

BEAUTY and the BEAST

New York After Dark
by Webster Way

YOU FUCKING PUNK.

I DID YOU A FAVOR BY ASKING YOU TO DO ME ONE, AND *THIS* IS WHAT I GET IN RETURN?

SOEFFER WAS STEAMED. TOO HOT TO EVEN NOTICE THAT *VICKI* WASN'T MENTIONED ON THE FRONT PAGE OF THE PAPER, WHERE KENNY'S MURDER WAS THE HEADLINE.

I PRAYED HE WASN'T THE *ONLY* ONE.

WHEN VICKI ASKED ME WHAT I'D *DONE,* IT WAS LIKE SHE WAS LOOKING FOR AN ANSWER THAT DIFFERED FROM THE TRUTH LYING AT HER *FEET.*

THERE WAS A SECOND, I THOUGHT I MIGHT HAVE TO *MAKE* HER UNDERSTAND-- NOT THE WHAT, BUT THE *WHY...*

BUT THAT PASSED.

SHE GOT IT.

AND THEN SHE *SOLD* IT...

97

BACK AT THE PARTY, IT WAS CLEAR FROM THE SMEAR ON BOTH OUR FACES WHAT WE'D BEEN *UP* TO...

IN THE BOATHOUSE VICKI SAID WE SHOULD BE DISCREET ABOUT LEAVING, WHILE AT THE SAME TIME MAKING SURE NOBODY MISSED OUR *EXIT*.

SHE SAID WE HAD TO BE ON EVERYONE'S LIPS UNTIL KENNY AND JAMES WERE FOUND, AND THEN...

...WE *STILL* HAD TO BE. SO THAT WHEN THE COPS STARTED LOOKING FOR ANSWERS...

...THERE WAS *NO* QUESTION ABOUT *US*.

US. SHE SAID *US*.

THAT WAS ALL I NEEDED TO HEAR.

SOEFFER HAD NO IDEA HOW GOOD A SALESMAN I WAS, TOO BUSY RATTLIN' ON ABOUT A WORTHLESS PIECE OF SHIT. I WASN'T LISTENIN'.

I JUST LOOKED AT HIS FEET. HIS CHEAP SHOES. THE CRUMBS IN HIS PANTS CUFFS.

NO FUCKIN' IDEA...

I HAD STOLEN THE MOST EXPENSIVE CAR ON THE LOT.

WHY DON'T YOU SHUT UP AN' FUCKING FIRE ME, OKAY?

WHY YOU...

LOOK, VICKI AND I...

IT WAS STUPID. FUCKING *STUPID.*

YOU DIDN'T USE YOUR *HEAD,* BOY.

AND NOW YOU'RE IN *TROUBLE...*

SHE TOLD ME *EVERY-THING.*

FIRING YOU IS THE *LAST* THING ON MY MIND.

YEAH?

THEN I *QUIT.*

HEHEHEH...

"...YOU CAN HAVE THE REST OF THE DAY *OFF.*"

CAN I BUY YOU A DRINK?

OPEN

I GOT MY OWN MONEY, THEO.

I'M SURE THAT'S TRUE, BUT MY OFFER IS FOR TOP SHELF...

WE GOT ONE SHELF.

CAN YOU MAKE A MARTINI?

I CAN PUT GIN IN A GLASS, WIT' SOME VERMOUTH.

OLIVES?

I THINK SO...

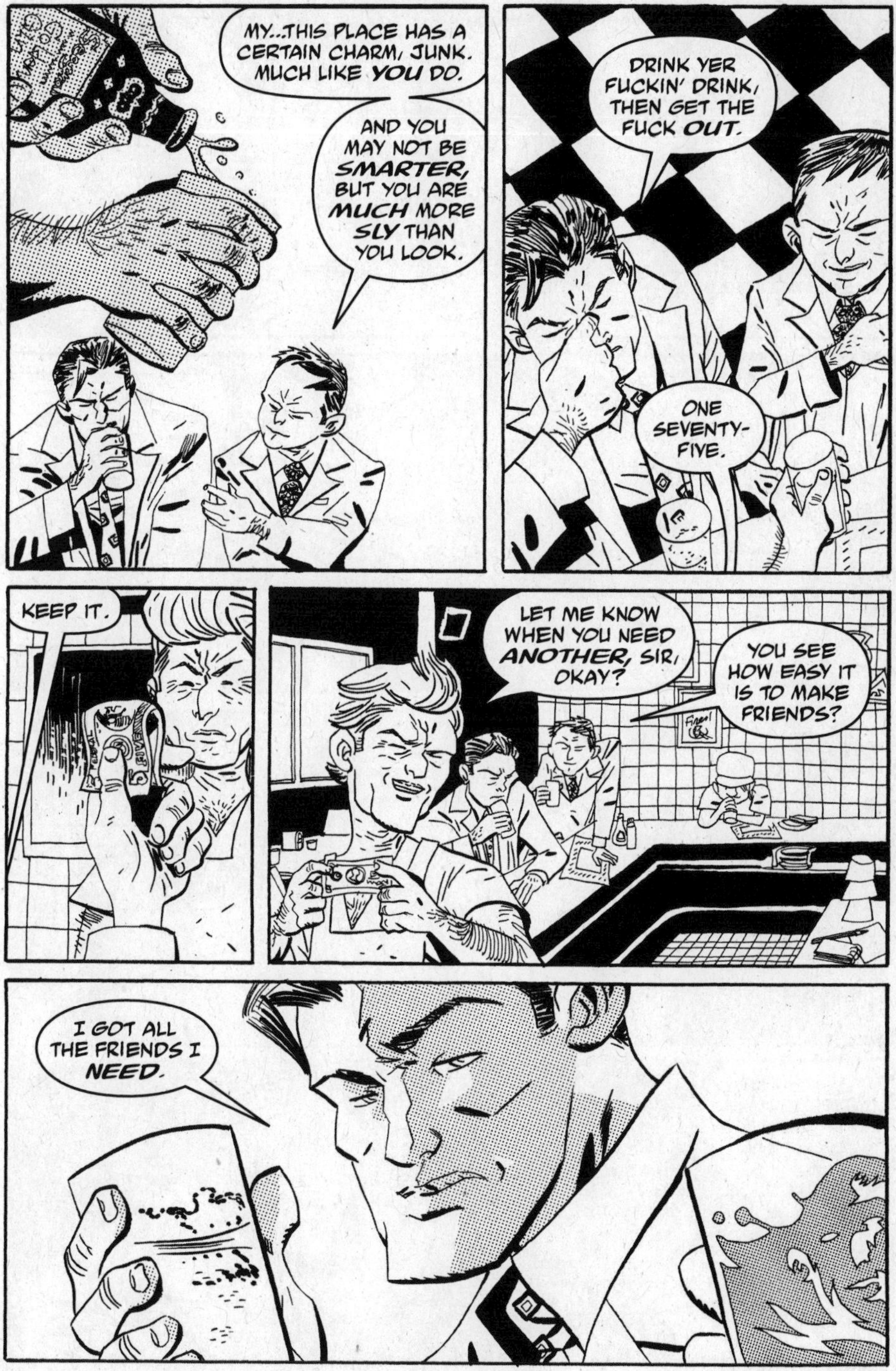

MY...THIS PLACE HAS A CERTAIN CHARM, JUNK. MUCH LIKE YOU DO.
AND YOU MAY NOT BE SMARTER, BUT YOU ARE MUCH MORE SLY THAN YOU LOOK.
DRINK YER FUCKIN' DRINK, THEN GET THE FUCK OUT.
ONE SEVENTY-FIVE.
KEEP IT.
LET ME KNOW WHEN YOU NEED ANOTHER, SIR, OKAY?
YOU SEE HOW EASY IT IS TO MAKE FRIENDS?
I GOT ALL THE FRIENDS I NEED.

I'M SURE *KENNY* THOUGHT THE SAME. THAT POOR BOY MADE A FRIEND OUT OF *ANYONE...*

...INCLUDING *THE ONE WHO KILLED* HIM.

ANY IDEA WHO THAT *WAS?*

YES, AND NO DOUBT WE'LL ALL FIND OUT SOON *ENOUGH,* ONCE HE'S FOUND.

YOU DIDN'T KNOW? BUT OF COURSE NOT--YOU AND VICKI *LEFT* BEFORE THE EXCITEMENT.

JAMES IS A FUGITIVE...

I IMAGINE THE COUPLE I SAW RUNNING OUT OF THE BOATHOUSE EARLIER ARE, *TOO*...

...I'M SORRY.

I DIDN'T *TELL* YOU BECAUSE...

--YOU DIDN'T WANT ME TO *KNOW.*

NO...YEAH. BUT CHARLENE, NO ONE WAS S'POSED TO. SOEFFER HIRED ME TO KEEP MY EYES ON HIS DAUGHTER...

YOU THREW IN THE *HANDS* FOR *FREE,* THEN?

I *DESERVE* THAT, I GUESS. BUT YOU DON'T--

I DON'T *WHAT?*

AND IF YOU DARE SAY *UNDERSTAND,* I'LL--

HEY!

I WASN'T LYING, I *DID* DESERVE THE COLD SHOULDER I WAS GETTIN' FROM CHARLENE.

BUT ALSO, I WOULD HAVE LIKED TO BE *LISTEN'D* TO...

JUNK!

I AIN'T IN THE MOOD FER YER *SHIT,* VINNY.

SHIT? WE AIN'T GOT *THAT* FOR YOU...

PUT 'ER THERE...

SNIFF
SNIFF

WHAT THE FUCK ARE YOU *DOIN'*?

SHAME...

HE DONE *WASHED HIS HAND,* FELLAS...

GIVE IT UP, JUNK--TELL US WHAT WAS IT LIKE!

FUCKIN' HIGH CLASS PIECE A' *PUSSY* LIKE THAT--YOU DOG!

AW...

DON'T HOLD OUT ON US, CASANOVA-- *SPILL!*

I GOT NOTHIN' TO SAY...

JUNK...

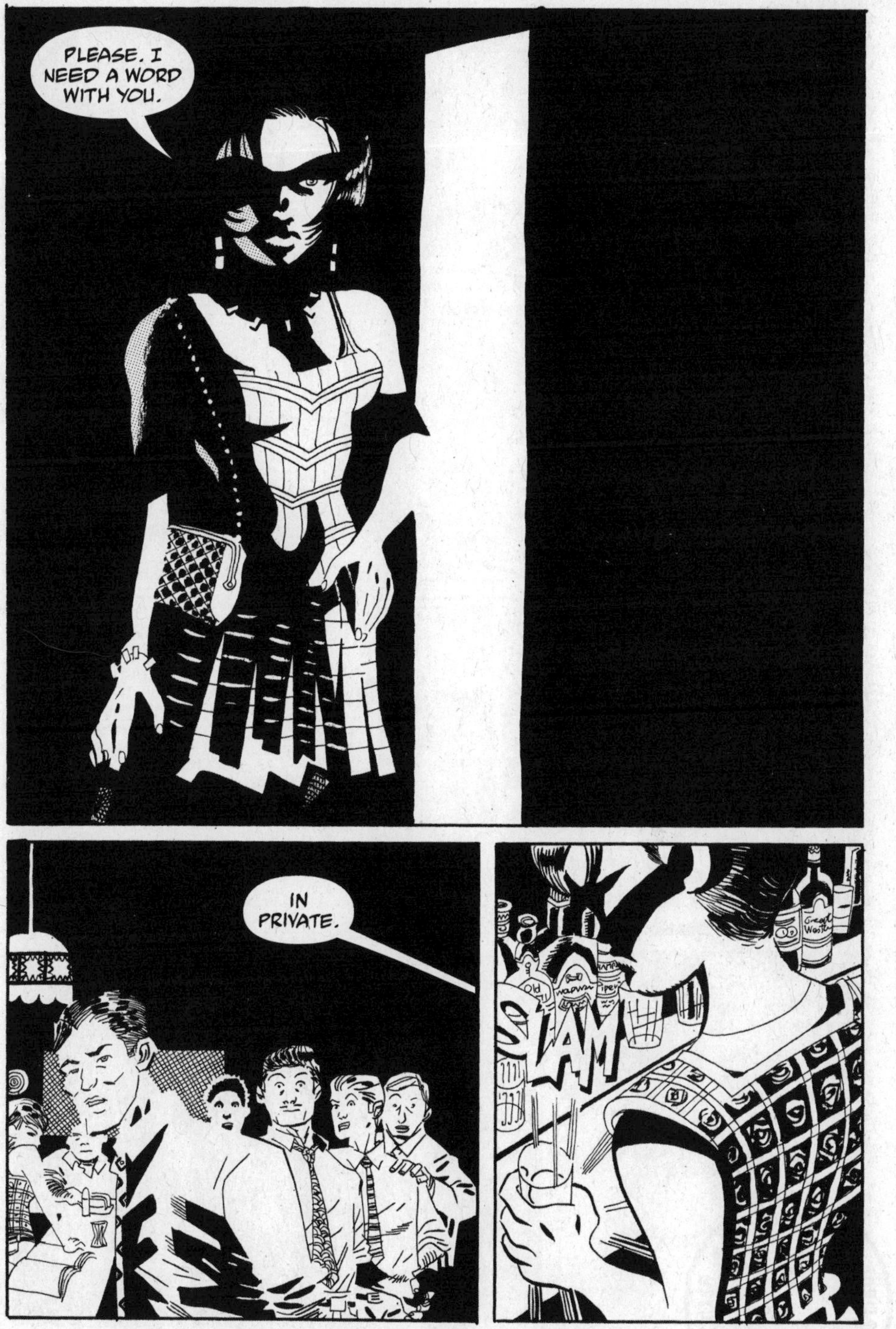
PLEASE. I NEED A WORD WITH YOU.
IN PRIVATE.
SLAM

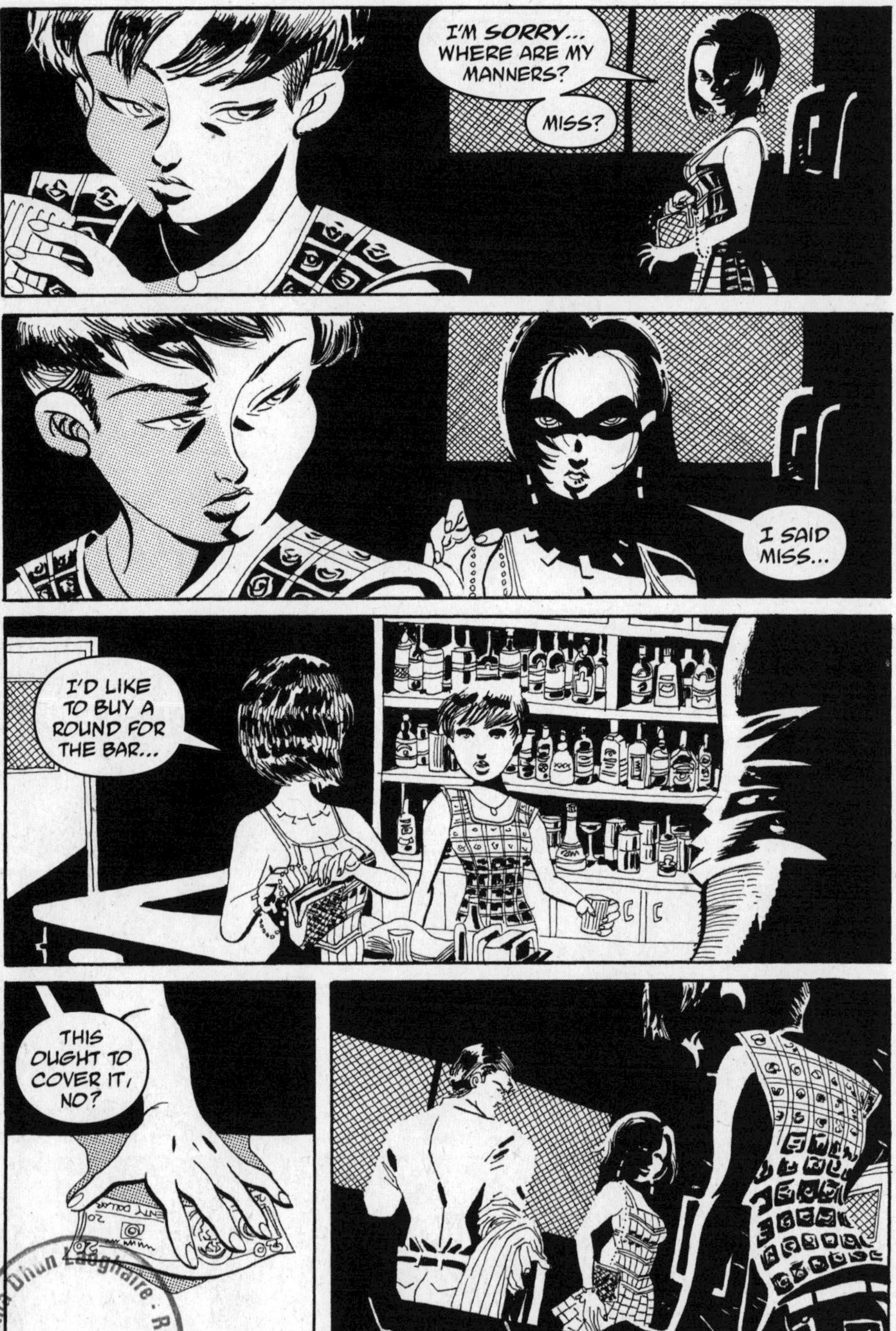
I'M SORRY... WHERE ARE MY MANNERS?
MISS?
I SAID MISS...
I'D LIKE TO BUY A ROUND FOR THE BAR...
THIS OUGHT TO COVER IT, NO?

I THOUGHT YOU SHOULD KNOW...I SPOKE WITH MY *FATHER*--

AND, WELL, I CONVINCED HIM THAT YOU WERE RIGHT.

I'M NOT YOUR *JOB* ANYMORE.

NOW *WAIT* A MINUTE--

JUNK--I UNDERSTAND. YOU'RE BEING SMART. WE *SHOULDN'T* SEE EACH OTHER ANYMORE. NOT AFTER...

I PRAY YOU'LL *FORGIVE* ME SOME DAY.

111

... I'VE TAKEN A ROOM AT THE PARAMOUNT HOTEL.

YER **OLD MAN** THROW YOU OUT?

WHAT? NO.

NEVER.

EVER. I JUST HAVE TO GET AWAY FROM...

HIM?

EVERYTHING.

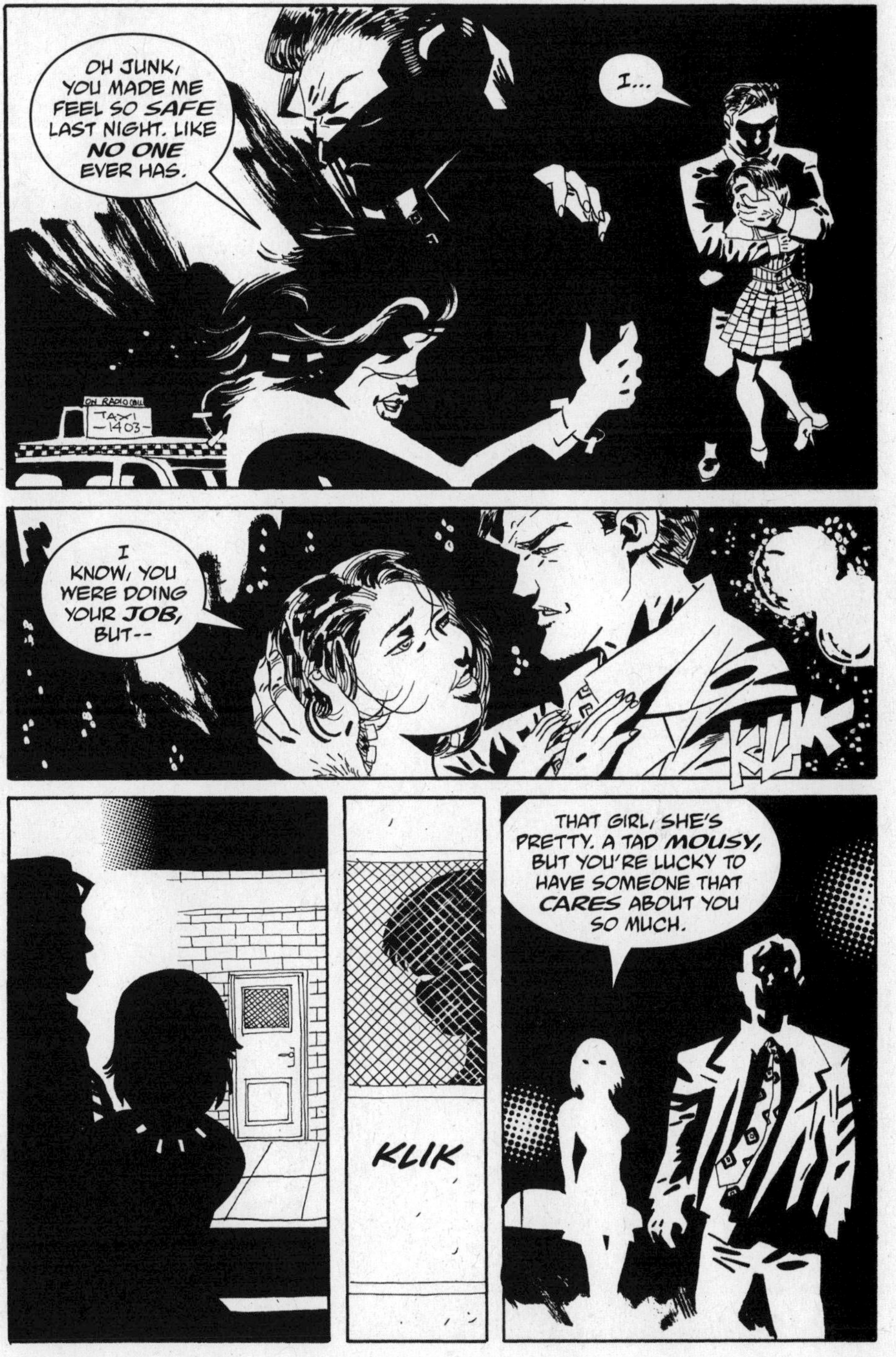
OH JUNK, YOU MADE ME FEEL SO SAFE LAST NIGHT. LIKE NO ONE EVER HAS.
I...
TAXI -1403-
I KNOW, YOU WERE DOING YOUR JOB, BUT--
KLIK
KLIK
THAT GIRL, SHE'S PRETTY. A TAD MOUSY, BUT YOU'RE LUCKY TO HAVE SOMEONE THAT CARES ABOUT YOU SO MUCH.

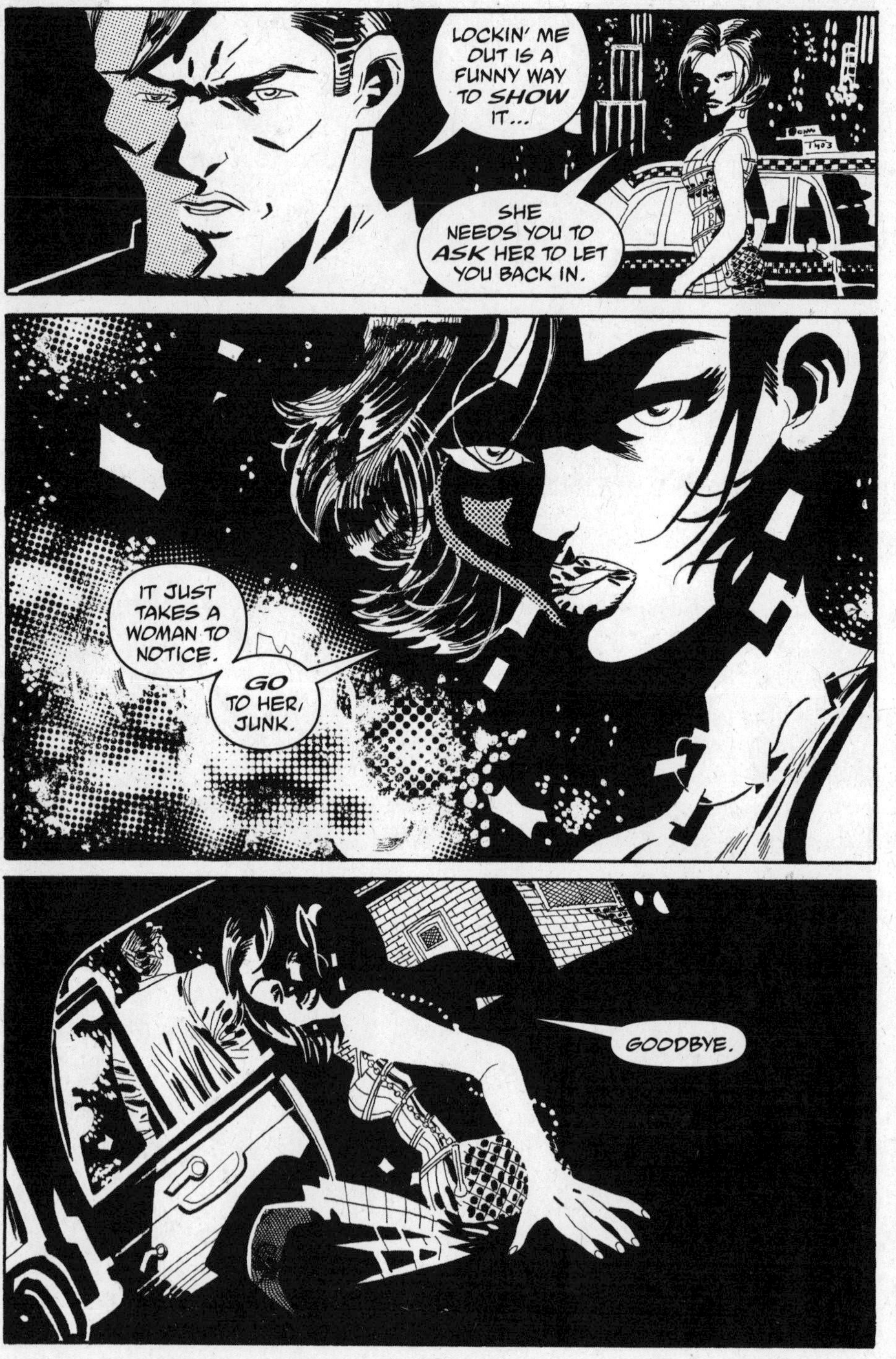
LOCKIN' ME OUT IS A FUNNY WAY TO SHOW IT...
SHE NEEDS YOU TO ASK HER TO LET YOU BACK IN.
IT JUST TAKES A WOMAN TO NOTICE.
GO TO HER, JUNK.
GOODBYE.

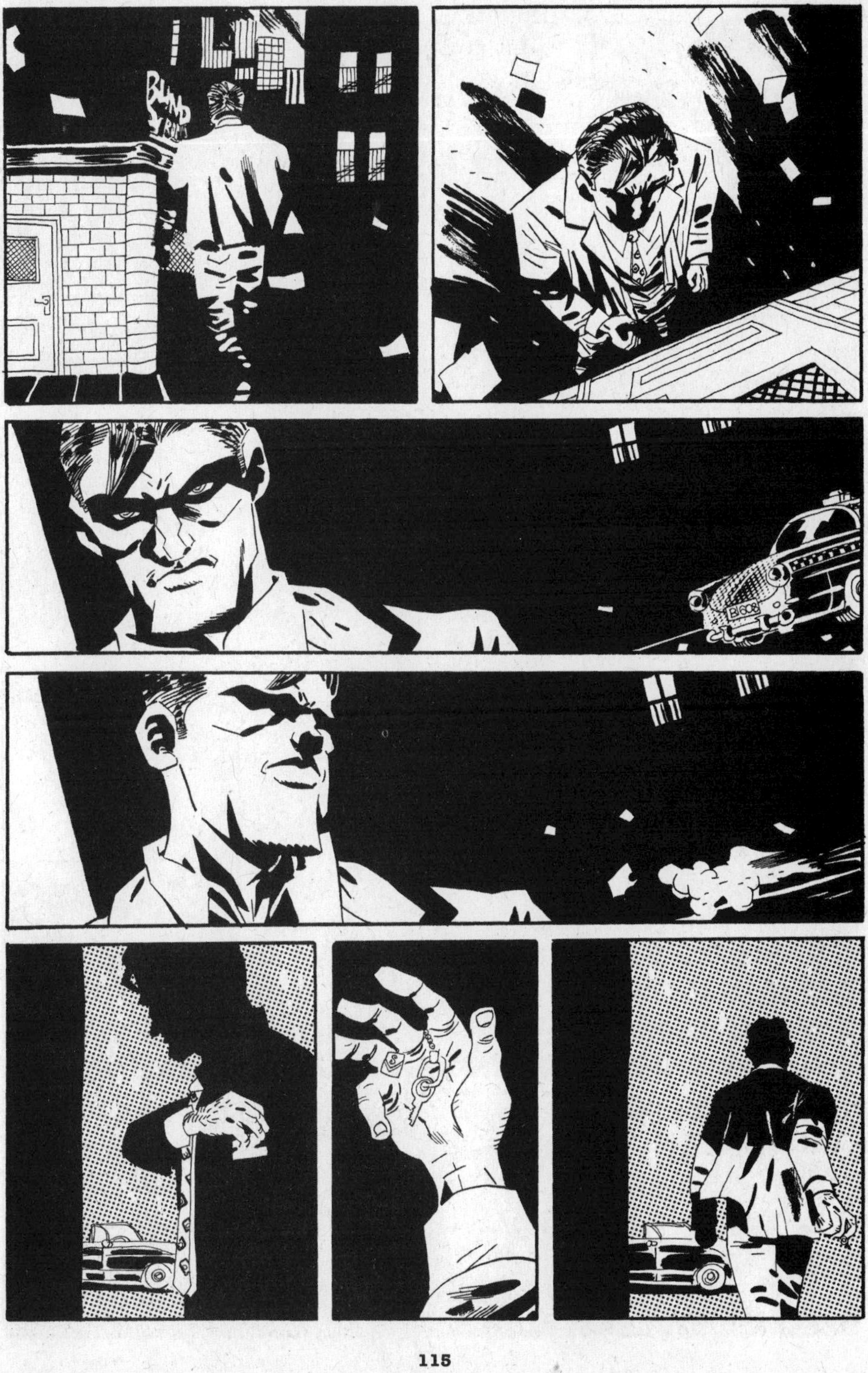

JUNK?

WHY ARE YOU?...

WHAT'S WRONG?

...I DON'T KNOW.

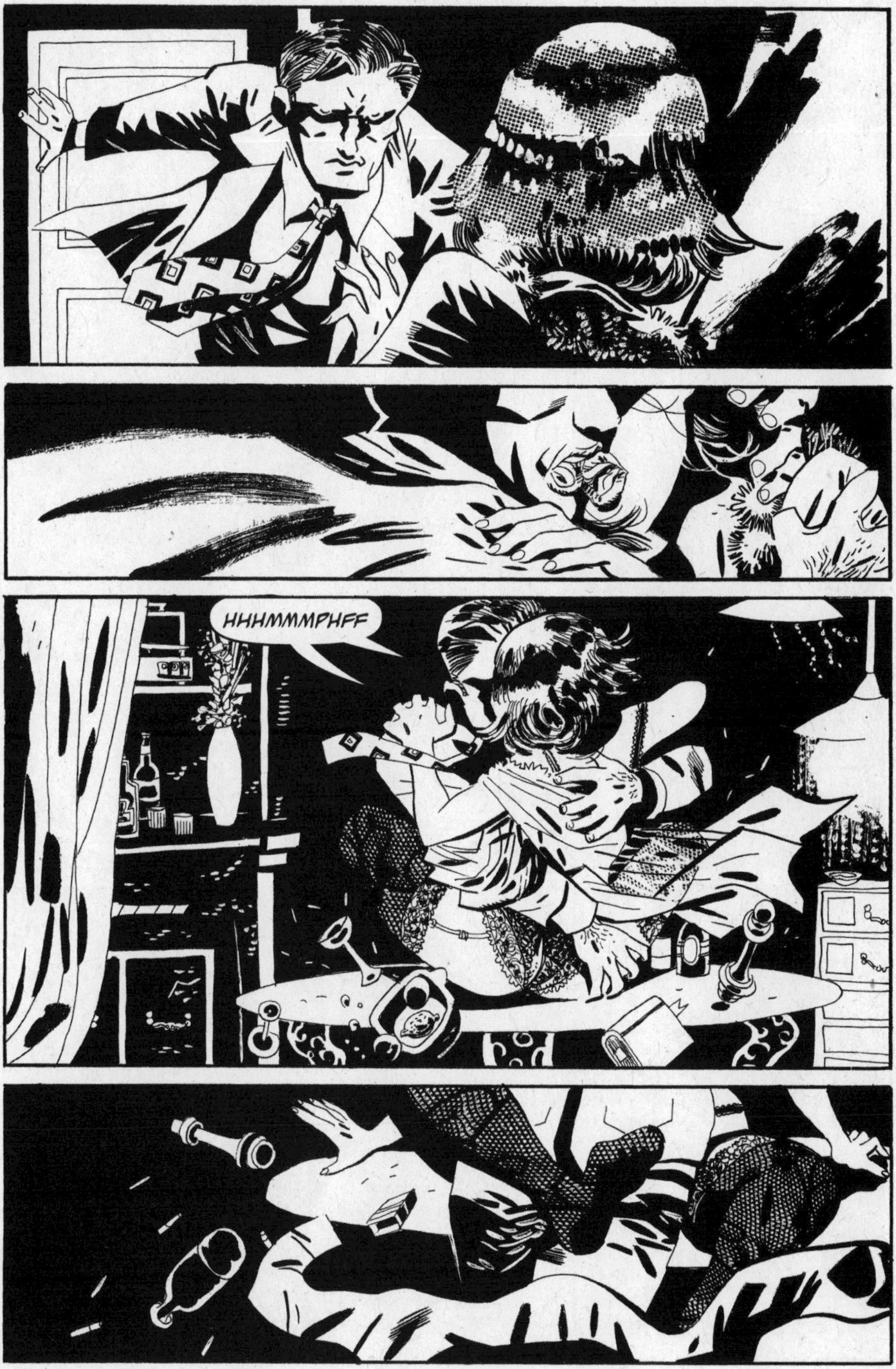
HHHMMMPHFF

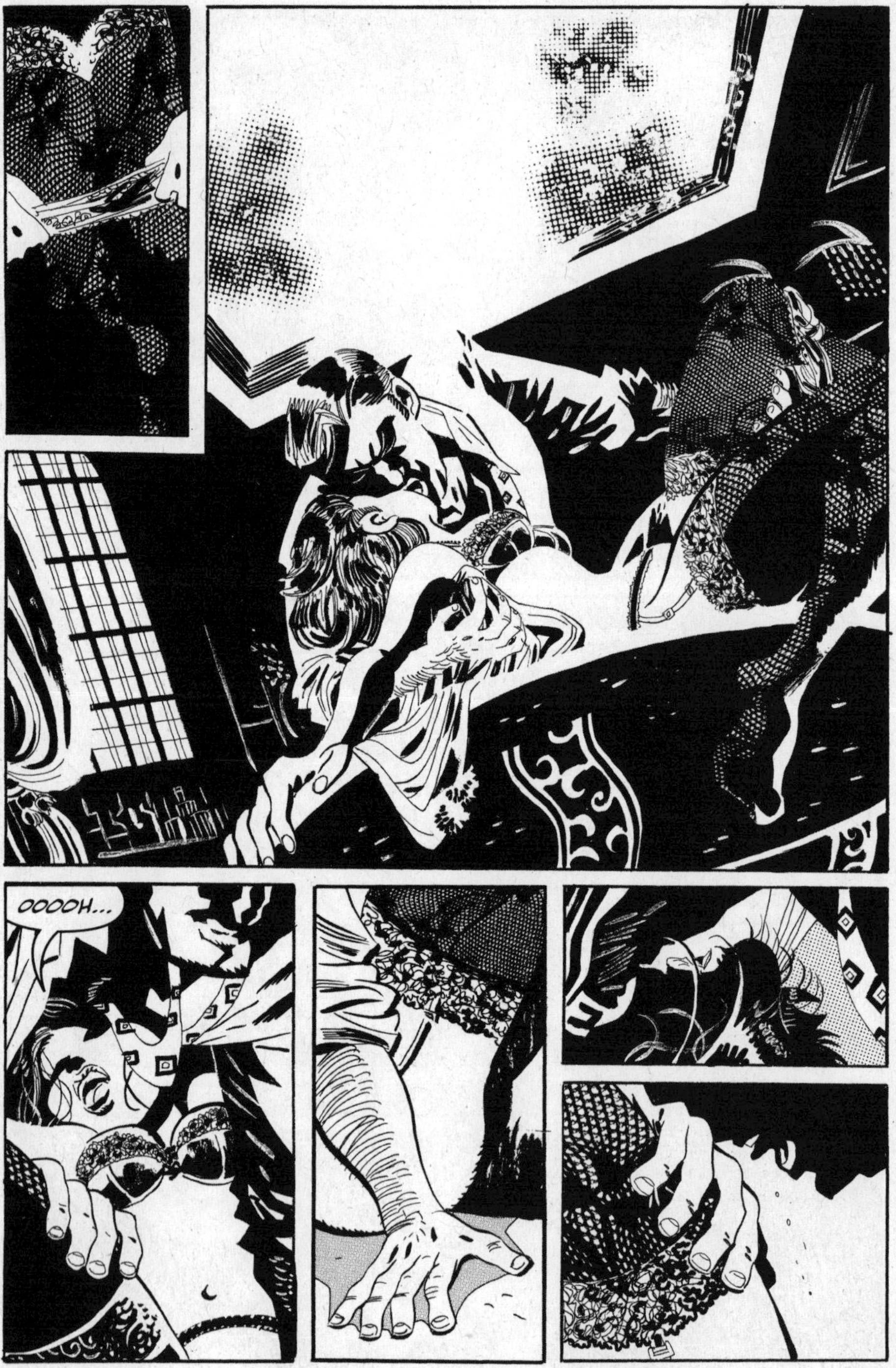
OOOOH...

SO BIG...

I KNEW IT.

UHHH

NO...
DON'T...

NOT YET...

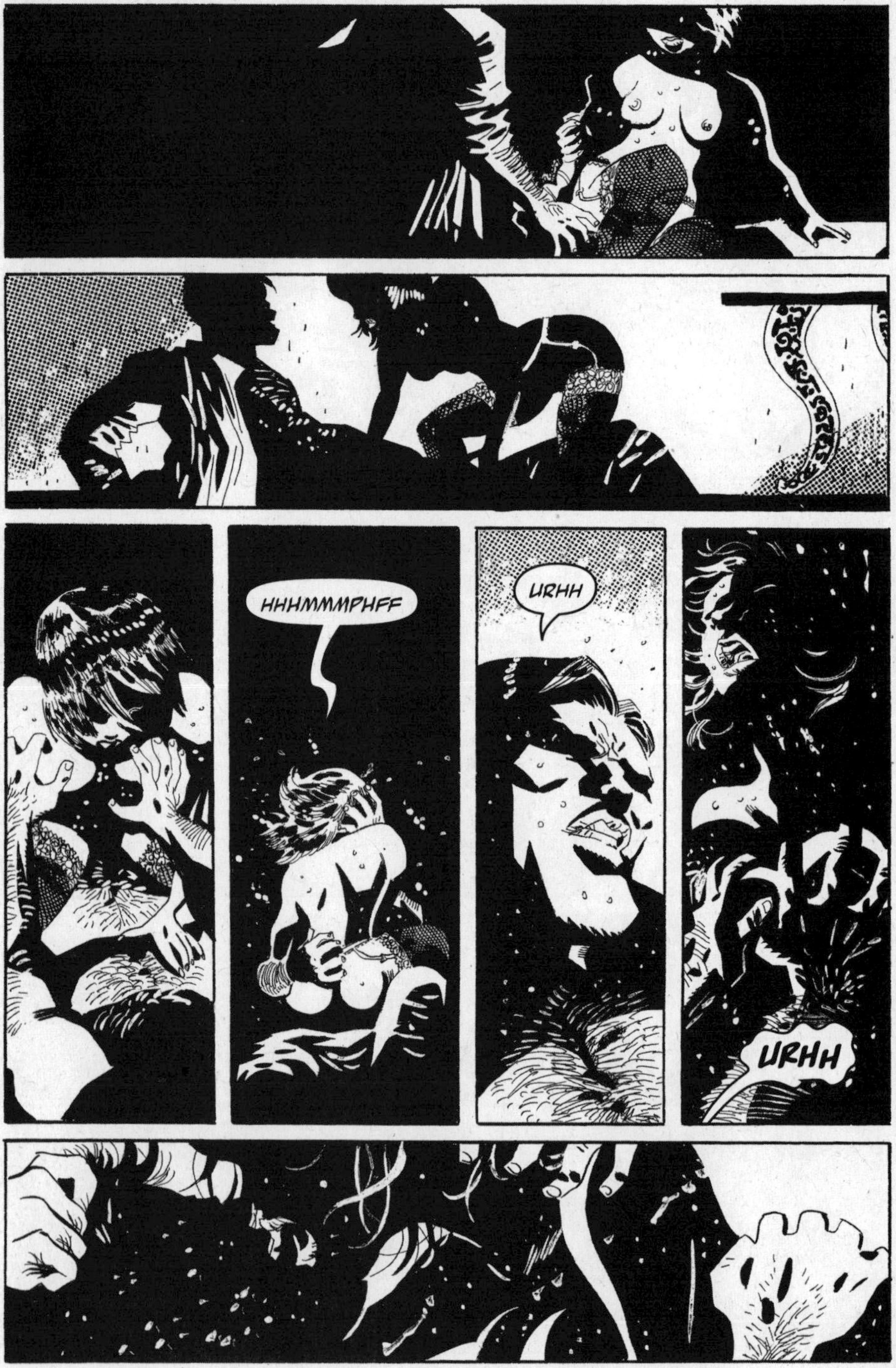
HHHMMMPHFF
URHH
URHH

SO I WAS THINKING...

YOU WERE *WHAT?*

THINKING.

I KNOW THIS SWELL LITTLE PLACE ON THE SHORE, WE CAN JUMP IN THE CAR, BE THERE BY DINNER TIME.

JUST *US.* AFTER EVERYTHING, Y'KNOW, JUST...

GO *AWAY* FOR A LITTLE BIT.

HOW'S *THAT* SOUND?

KNOCK KNOCK

LIKE SOMETHING MY *FATHER* WOULDN'T APPROVE.

THE HELL WITH HIM.

WATCH YER *EYES*, FRIEND.

JUNK... HE TAKES *CARE* OF ME. I *NEED* MY DADDY.

AND I NEED *YOU*...

LEAVE DADDY TO ME.

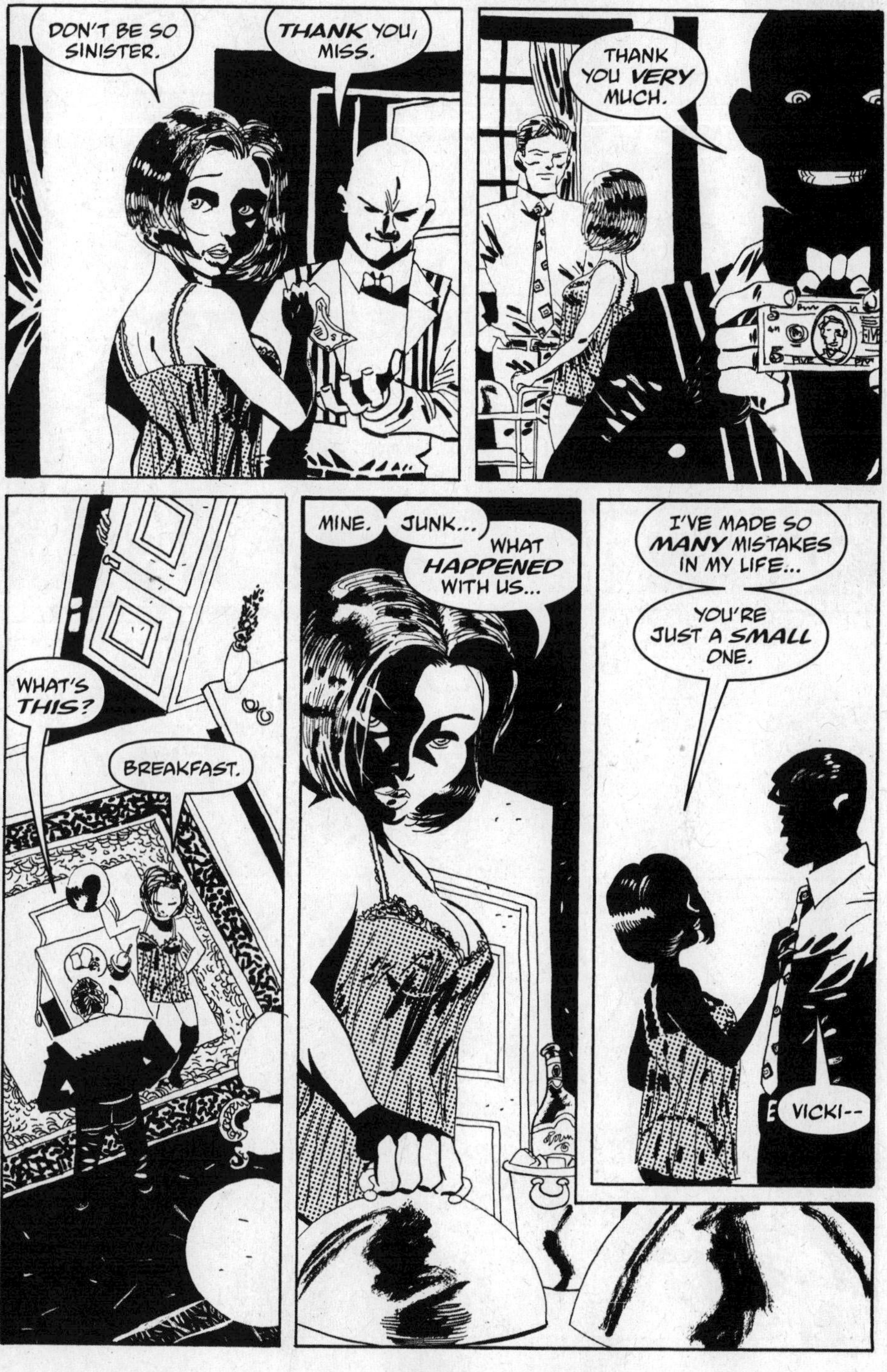

DON'T BE SO SINISTER.
THANK YOU, MISS.
THANK YOU VERY MUCH.
WHAT'S THIS?
BREAKFAST.
MINE.
JUNK...
WHAT HAPPENED WITH US...
I'VE MADE SO MANY MISTAKES IN MY LIFE...
YOU'RE JUST A SMALL ONE.
VICKI--

IT WOULD BE *UNFAIR* OF ME TO EXPECT YOU TO UNDERSTAND, I KNOW. YOU AND I, WE'RE FROM DIFFERENT...

I CAN'T KEEP MY *HANDS* OFF YOU. WHEN I SAW YOU DANCING WITH SALLY-- IT DROVE ME TO THE BOATHOUSE. I...

YOU...

YOU SHOULD *GO.*

VICKI...

GO!

I MEAN, I KNOW MY *WAY* AROUND A WOMAN'S BODY.

AND I KNEW *SHE* KNEW THAT, TOO.

I LEFT. I WON'T KID, I WAS *SORE.* I'M SURE *VICKI* WAS, TOO...

BUT WHAT SHE *DIDN'T* KNOW, SHE DIDN'T *WANT* TO. THERE WAS MORE TO ME THAT SHE WAS AFRAID OF. AND MAYBE SHE WAS RIGHT TO FEEL THAT WAY.

MAYBE SHE SAW SOMETHING IN ME I DIDN'T KNOW WAS *THERE.* OR MAYBE...

...SHE WAS *WRONG.*

MAYBE I SHOULDN'T HAVE TRIED TO FIND *OUT.* MAYBE...

I WAS WRONG.

POP

HEY!

DON'T PLAY **ROUGH** WITH US, LOVERBOY, ALL WE WANT IS A PICTURE!

THEN WHY DON'CHA **ASK** FIRST!?

MIND IF WE?...

THE **KIT KAT KLUB**

FEATURING JAZZ AND SOUL

POP POP

POP POP

POP POP

THERE'S NO FORGIVIN' THE LIE YER LIVIN'...♪

LOOKING FOR SOME-THING...

JUNK?

NO, SALLY...

I GOT ALL I NEED RIGHT HERE.

HEH. SPOKEN LIKE EVERY DESPERATE SOUL THAT HOLDS AN EMPTY GLASS.

C'MON, *THAT* WHAT YOU THINK I AM?

ACTUALLY?

I THINK FOR A TALL MAN, YOU'RE IN *WAY* OVER YOUR HEAD.

I'M NOT SURE HOW TO RESPOND TO A LINE LIKE THAT...

THUS PROVING MY POINT.

LOOK, ABOUT THE OTHER NIGHT...

WHICH NIGHT?

THEY ALL SEEM TO BLEND TOGETHER, AND THE COLD LIGHT OF DAY ISN'T CHILLING *ENOUGH* TO DISTINGUISH ONE FROM THE OTHER.

YOU'RE LUCKY I EVEN REMEMBER YOUR NAME.

WELL, THAT MAKES ME *SOMETHING*, ANYWAY.

IS *THAT* WHAT YOU WANT TO BE?

I USED TO THINK SOMETHING WAS *ENOUGH*...

BUT THEN I BECAME *SOME-BODY*.

AND LET ME *TELL* YOU-- BEING *SOMEBODY* IS A *FULL TIME JOB*.

YOU DON'T WANT THAT. AND IF YOU *DO*, YOU *SHOULDN'T*.

I CAN GET YOU *WORK*, THOUGH. A MAN LIKE YOU...

I KNOW DIRECTORS... THEY'RE *ALWAYS* LOOKING FOR *STUNT-MEN.* IF YOU WOULD MOVE TO CALIFORNIA, I'D PUT IN A GOOD WORD.

WHY WOULD YOU DO THAT FOR *ME?*

MAYBE I HAVE A SOFT SPOT FOR *LOST CAUSES.*

OH, SO THAT'S WHAT YOU THINK I AM.

WELL, LET ME SHOW YOU HOW WRONG YOU...

MISS PETRI?

I HAVE TO GO.

THINK ABOUT IT, JUNK.

OR DON'T.

THE LIE YER LIVIN', IS TRUE AS I CAN BE!

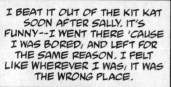

I BEAT IT OUT OF THE KIT KAT SOON AFTER SALLY. IT'S FUNNY--I WENT THERE 'CAUSE I WAS BORED, AND LEFT FOR THE SAME REASON. I FELT LIKE WHEREVER I WAS, IT WAS THE WRONG PLACE.

LIKE I WAS *MISSING* SOMETHING, SOMEWHERE.

JUNK...

JAMES? WHAT ARE--

I NEED TO *TALK* TO YOU...

ABOUT THE OTHER NIGHT.

SHHH, SSHH, KEEP IT DOWN...

KEEP IT *DOWN?* YOU KNOW WHAT THEY SAY I *DID?*

YOU DON'T REMEMBER?

NO.

NOTHING?

I REMEMBER WAKING *UP*...SEEING *KENNY,* ALL THE BLOOD...

MY *PANTS*... HE MUST HAVE *TRIED* SOMETHING-- I NEVER KNEW HE WAS LIKE THAT...

I WAS HIGH...

YOU GOTTA **HELP** ME!

OKAY, OKAY...HOLD IT TOGETHER.

YOU'VE BEEN IN TROUBLE BEFORE--WHAT SHOULD I **DO**?

WELL, TURNING YOURSELF **IN** MIGHT--

--BUY ME A TICKET TO **DEATH ROW**.

C'MON, A WEALTHY KID LIKE YOU?

WEALTHY? **THAT'S A RIOT.** I GOT **NOTHIN'**.

EVERY TIME I CALL HOME, MY FATHER HANGS **UP**.

WHAT'S YER OLD MAN **DO**, ANYWAY?

HE COUNTS HIS BLESSINGS.

ALL RIGHT. I CAN GET YOU OUT OF *TOWN*, MAYBE--

CAN YOU?

MAYBE. BUT I NEED YOU TO LAY *LOW*...

AND BE THERE--AT *ALL* TIMES. YOU DON'T COME OUT *NO MORE*, UNDERSTAN' ME?

YEAH, YEAH SURE. I'M STAYIN' AT THE *SQUARE ARMS*.

THAT *FLOP HOUSE* ON FORTY-EIGHT?

LIKE I SAID, I GOT *NOTHIN'*...

BUT *YOU,*

ABOUT THAT...

I SAW *VICKI* TONIGHT...

"...SHE SAID YOU MIGHT BE HERE."

WELL, WELL...SEEMS I WASN'T WRONG ABOUT YOU IN THE *LEAST*...

GALAHAD.

YOU REALLY ARE *QUITE* A KNIGHT.

I DON'T KNOW WHAT YER *TALKIN'* ABOUT, MR. WAY.

DO YOU KNOW WHAT I *HEARD*, MR. JUNKIN?...

I HEARD IT *ALL*.

THAT'S TOO BAD. THE SQUARE ARMS IS A LOUSY PLACE FOR THE *END OF THE ROAD.*

JUNK-- I HAVE *NO* INTENTION OF TURNING JAMES OVER TO THE POLICE.

FUGITIVES, THEY SELL *PAPERS.*

DO US BOTH A FAVOR, AND *KEEP* HIM ONE AS LONG AS YOU CAN.

IT'LL BE WORTH YOUR *WHILE.*

WEBSTER WAY'S WORDS *HAUNTED* ME ALL THE LONG LONELY DRIVE I TOOK TO THE SHORE.

I'D HEARD THEM BEFORE-- IN SOUTH BEND, FROM SOME... BUSINESSMEN WHO'D COME FROM CHICAGO.

THE SECOND IT TURNS TO *TROUBLE.*

"WE'LL MAKE IT WORTH YOUR WHILE." THE TROUBLE WITH A *WHILE* IS, IT AIN'T LONG. IT COMES TO AN *END...*

AND THOUGH I COULDN'T SEE IT COMING, I KNEW...

TROUBLE WAS JUST OVER THE HORIZON. SO WHY SHOULDN'T I BE THINKING ABOUT PUTTING SOME *DISTANCE* BETWEEN ME AND IT?

CALIFORNIA...

HOME MADE ICE CREAM

ICE CREAM

A STUNTMAN... WELL, THAT COULD BE A *START*--AND LEAD TO BETTER THINGS. A GUY LIKE ME? IF HE PUTS HIS MIND TO IT, HE GETS NOTICED, ONLY A MATTER OF *TIME*...

LEAVE ALL THE *LOST CAUSE* FAKES AND PHONIES *BEHIND.*

?

WHERE HAVE YOU **BEEN**, JUNK?

VICKI... HOW'D YOU GET IN MY **ROOM**?

WHY JUNK...

SLAM

THERE'S NOT A DOOR IN THIS CITY THAT **WON'T** OPEN FOR A PRETTY GIRL.

NO...

I SUPPOSE NOT.

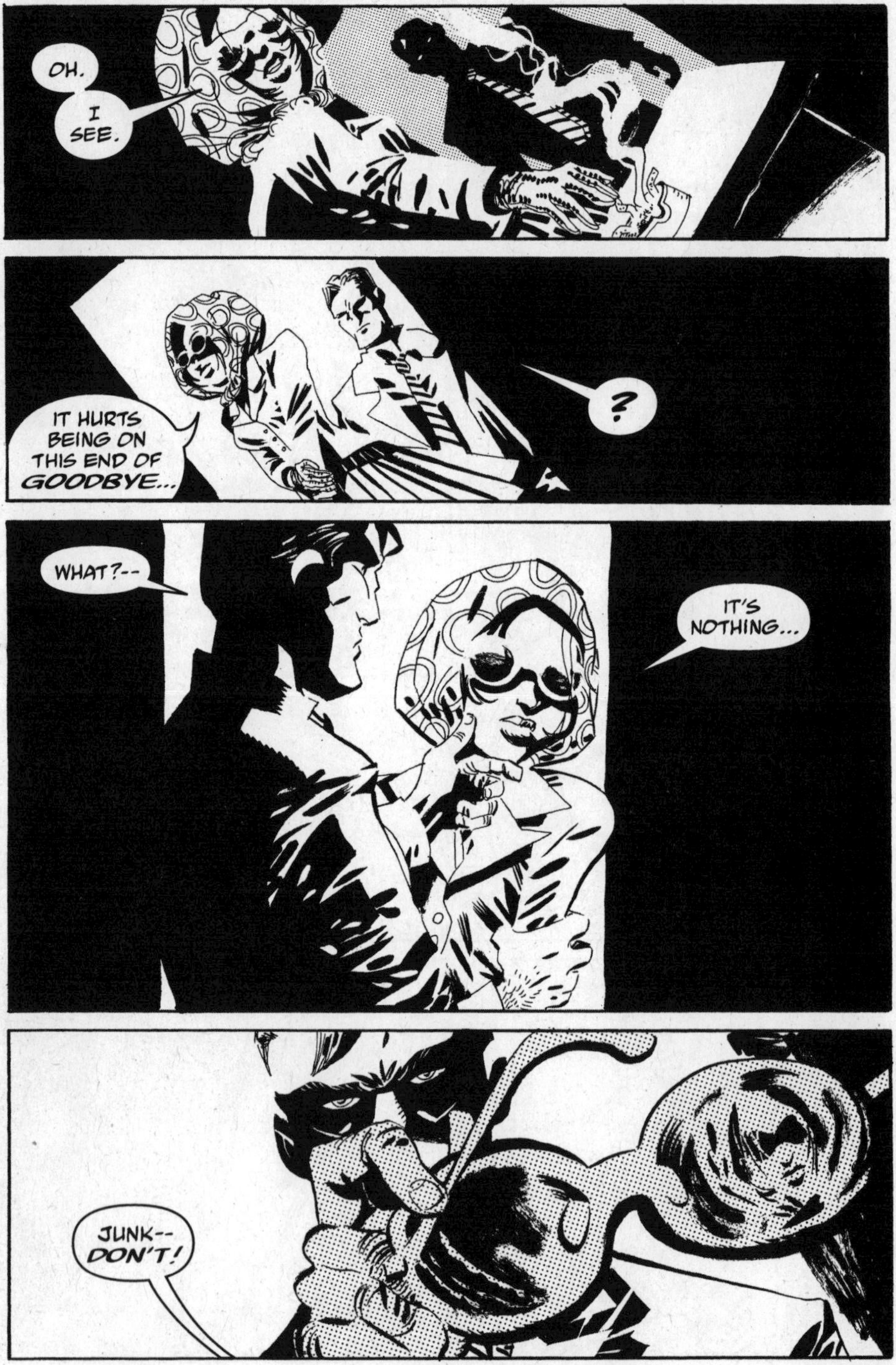
OH.
I SEE.
IT HURTS BEING ON THIS END OF GOODBYE...
?
WHAT?--
IT'S NOTHING...
JUNK-- DON'T!

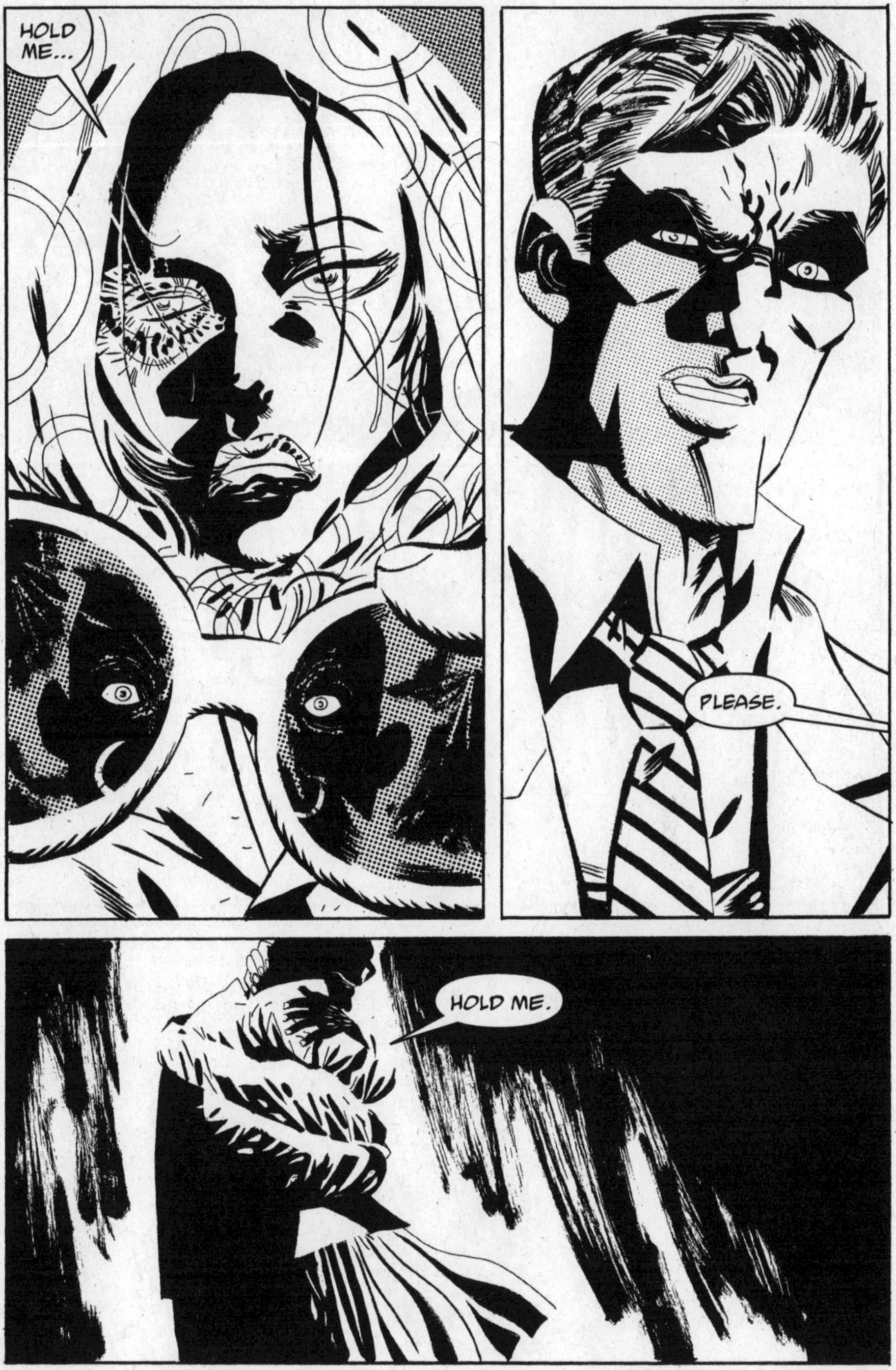
HOLD ME...
PLEASE.
HOLD ME.

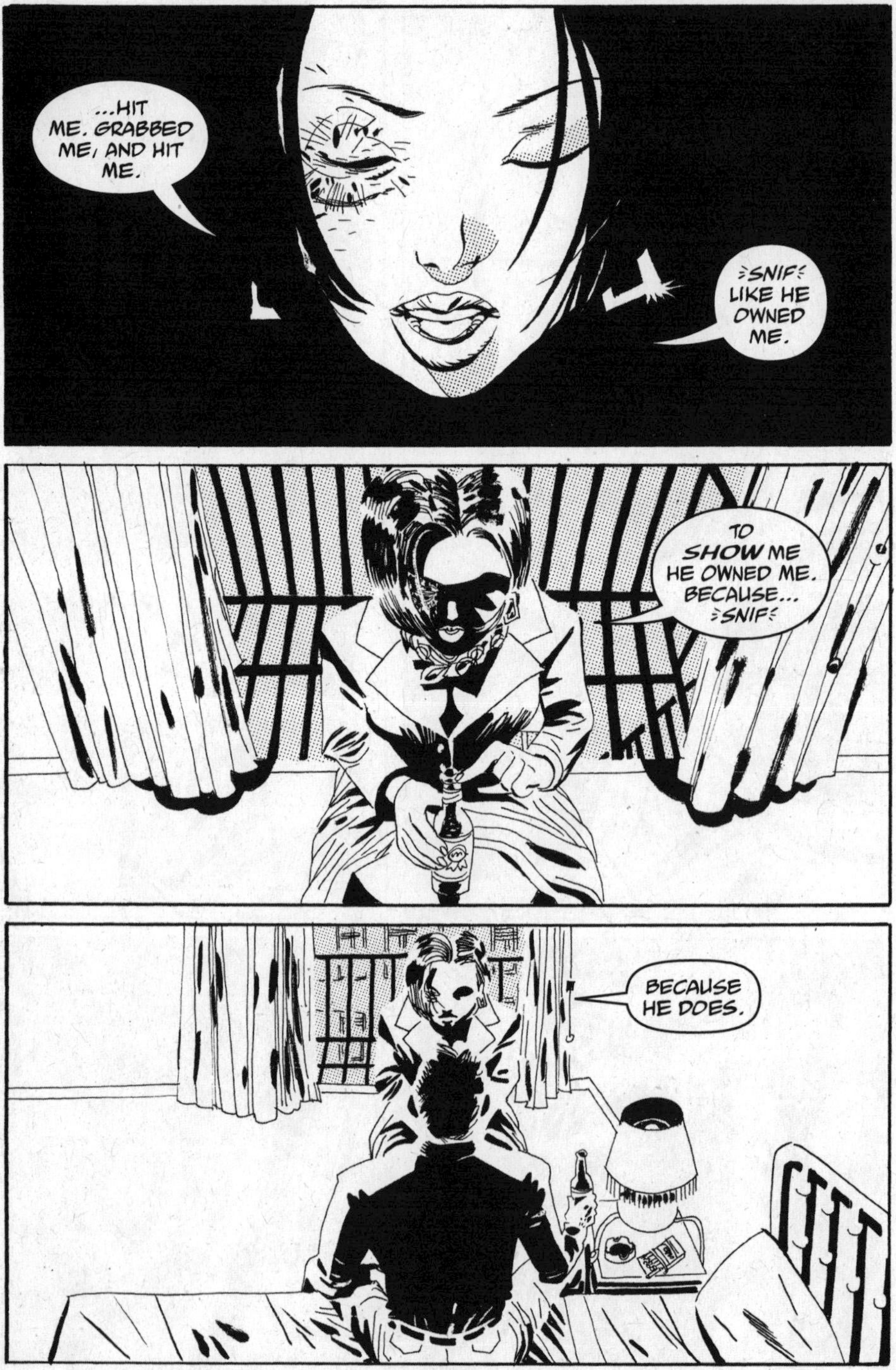

...HIT ME. GRABBED ME, AND HIT ME.
SNIF LIKE HE OWNED ME.
TO SHOW ME HE OWNED ME. BECAUSE... SNIF
BECAUSE HE DOES.

LIKE HELL.

NO JUNK, IT'S SO MUCH WORSE. HELL IS SOMETHING THAT'S *EARNED* AFTER A LONG LIFE OF INDISCRETIONS AND STUBBORNNESS...

ALL I DID WAS BE BORN UNDER HIS ROOF.

DO YOU KNOW WHY MY FATHER HIRED YOU?

TO KEEP YOU OUT OF THE PAPERS. YOU WERE BAD FOR BUSINESS.

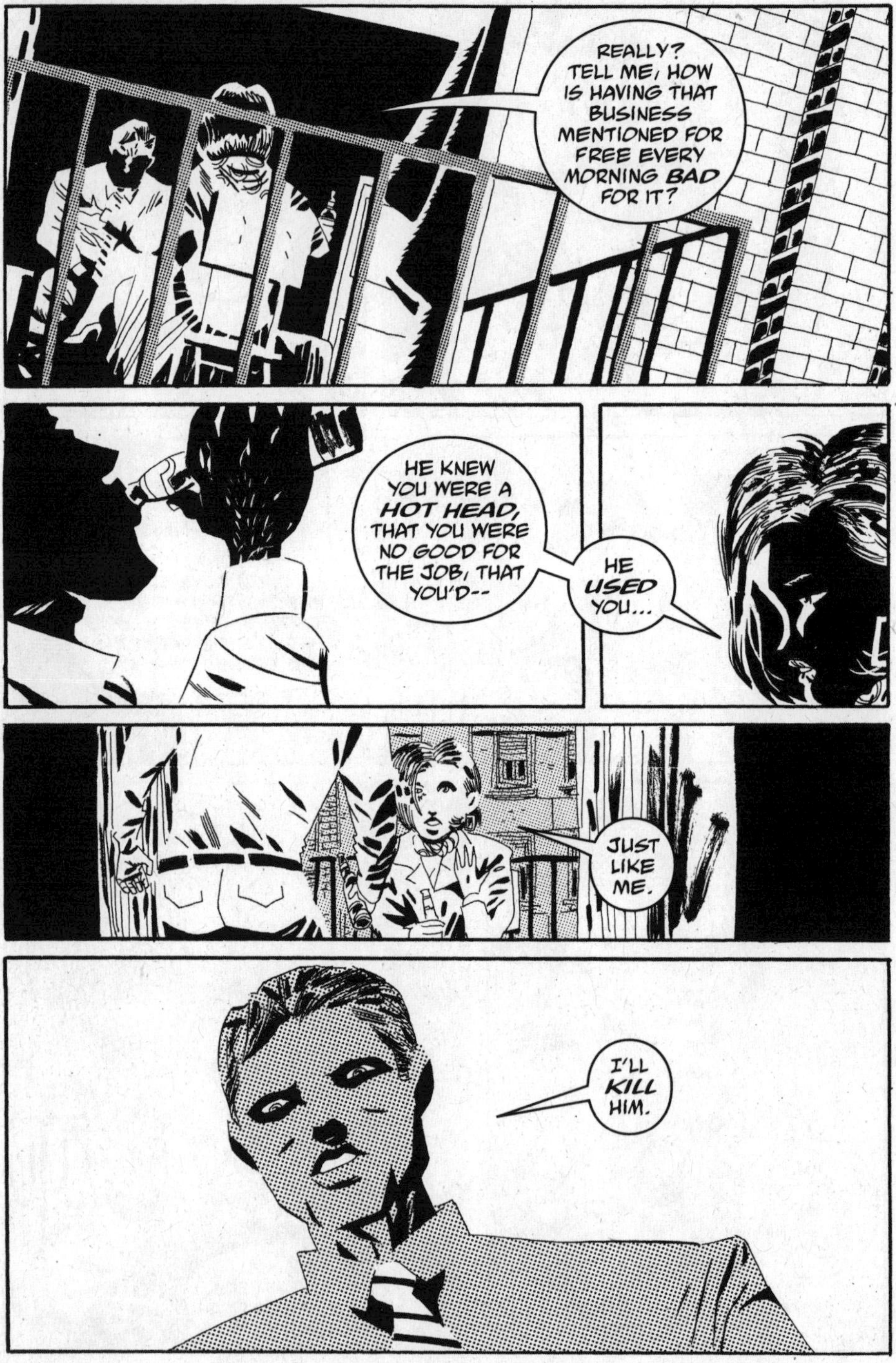
REALLY? TELL ME, HOW IS HAVING THAT BUSINESS MENTIONED FOR FREE EVERY MORNING BAD FOR IT?
HE KNEW YOU WERE A HOT HEAD, THAT YOU WERE NO GOOD FOR THE JOB, THAT YOU'D--
HE USED YOU...
JUST LIKE ME.
I'LL KILL HIM.

I APPRECIATE THE OFFER, BUT NO. SEEING YOU IN THE *ELECTRIC CHAIR* WOULD BE MORE THAN I COULD BEAR.

I'M SORRY I SAID THAT.

YOU DIDN'T *MEAN* IT?

I'M *PISSED-- HOT*--TALKING OUT OF MY ASS.

MAYBE GIVE HIM A TASTE OF HIS OWN *MEDICINE?*

MY FATHER IS A *POWERFUL MAN*, WITH *STRONG FRIENDS...*

I COULDN'T BEAR TO SEE YOU IN A *WHEELCHAIR,* EITHER.

NO, I HAVE TO ACCEPT THAT I'M HIS *DAUGHTER,* AND AS SUCH...

MY BED IS MADE FOR ME.

SLAM

NO IT ISN'T! I CAN GET YOU *OUT* OF THIS!

HOW, *JUNK?* THE ONLY WAY IS-- WE CAN'T EVEN *SAY* IT...

CALIFORNIA.

EXCUSE ME?

CALIFORNIA. LISTEN, I SAW SALLY LAST NIGHT.

YOU DID?

AND SHE OFFERED ME A JOB--IN THE MOVIES! WE CAN HAVE A LIFE OUT IN THE SUN--IT MIGHT BE TIGHT AT FIRST, BUT I'LL MAKE IT, BABY! YOU CAN *COUNT* ON ME!

I *KNOW* I CAN, JUNK DARLING, BUT...

...CAN WE COUNT ON *SALLY?*

YOU LET *ME* WORRY ABOUT THAT...

NO.

NO, NO, NO--WE SHOULD HAVE SOMETHING STRONGER.

ALL I GOT'S BEER, BABY.

CAN YOU GO OUT AND GET A BOTTLE AND MIXERS?

SURE. SURE, I CAN DO THAT.

AND MAYBE SOME SANDWICHES? I'M FAMISHED...DO YOU KNOW A PLACE?

PUP'S. IT'S THE BEST-- AND HE DOES CARRY-OUT, TOO...

"...I'LL KILL TWO BIRDS WITH ONE STONE."

SAY PUP, YOU EVER HAVE THAT FEELING THAT LIFE WAS PULLIN' UP ITS TROUSERS?

WHAT THE HELL YOU MEAN BY THAT?

THAT IT WAS DONE *SHITTING* ON YOU.

NO. NO, I *NEVER* GET THAT FEELING. BUT I FEEL SORRY FOR GUYS THAT *DO*.

WHY'S THAT?

'CAUSE THEY LOST TRACK A' WHERE THE SHIT'S REALLY *COMIN'* FROM.

YOU WANT *CHEESE* ON THIS?

HUH?

CHEESE.

SURE. SHE DON' EAT IT, I WILL.

SHE?

THEO, WHAT ARE *YOU* DOING HERE?

SLUMMING. AGAIN.

ENJOY THE *KING* OF BLEND

ACTUALLY, JUNK... THERE'S SOMEONE *ASKING* AFTER YOU...

NOT INTERESTED. MY DANCE CARD'S FULL TONIGHT.

OH. THAT'S A *SHAME.* *SALLY* WILL BE DISAPPOINTED.

SALLY?

YES. IT SEEMED *URGENT...*

WHAT HAPPENED TO THAT *DANCE CARD?*

I GUESS THE BAND'S ON *BREAK.* TOO BAD.

JUNK...

LISTEN. I THINK YOU'RE A GOOD KID. AND I THINK...

DON'T *BLAME* ME.

BLAME YOU? FER WHAT?

DOING MY JOB...

"...I'M JUST THE *MESSENGER*."

"*JUST THE MESSENGER?*" *BULLSHIT.* THEO WAS ONE OF *THOSE GUYS*--AND I WASN'T ABOUT TO LET HIM DO WHAT HE WANTED...

RUB ME THE *WRONG WAY.*

HE WAS AN *UPPER HAND* GUY--THE KIND THAT TRIED TO MAKE ME BELIEVE HE WAS *SMARTER* THAN ME.

SAME AS THAT SHIT BAG *MEECH.* AND I WAS *THROUGH* WITH THEM.

THEO COULD TAKE HIS UPPER HAND, AND SHOVE IT UP HIS *ASS.*

I WASN'T ABOUT TO LET HIM BOTHER ME. HELL, I COULDN'T. I HAD A GIRL BACK HOME...

...AND ONE WAITING IN A PLACE THAT *SURPRISED* ME.

KNOCK KNOCK

KNOCK KNOCK KNOCK KNOCK

YEAH?

IS *SALLY* IN THERE?

SLAM

155

NO, NO MAN, *AIN'T* NO SALLY HERE.

YOU SURE?

SURE I'M SURE--

YOU KNOW, I'VE BEEN *LIED* TO ENOUGH IN MY LIFE TO *KNOW* WHEN I'M BEING LIED TO.

HEY!

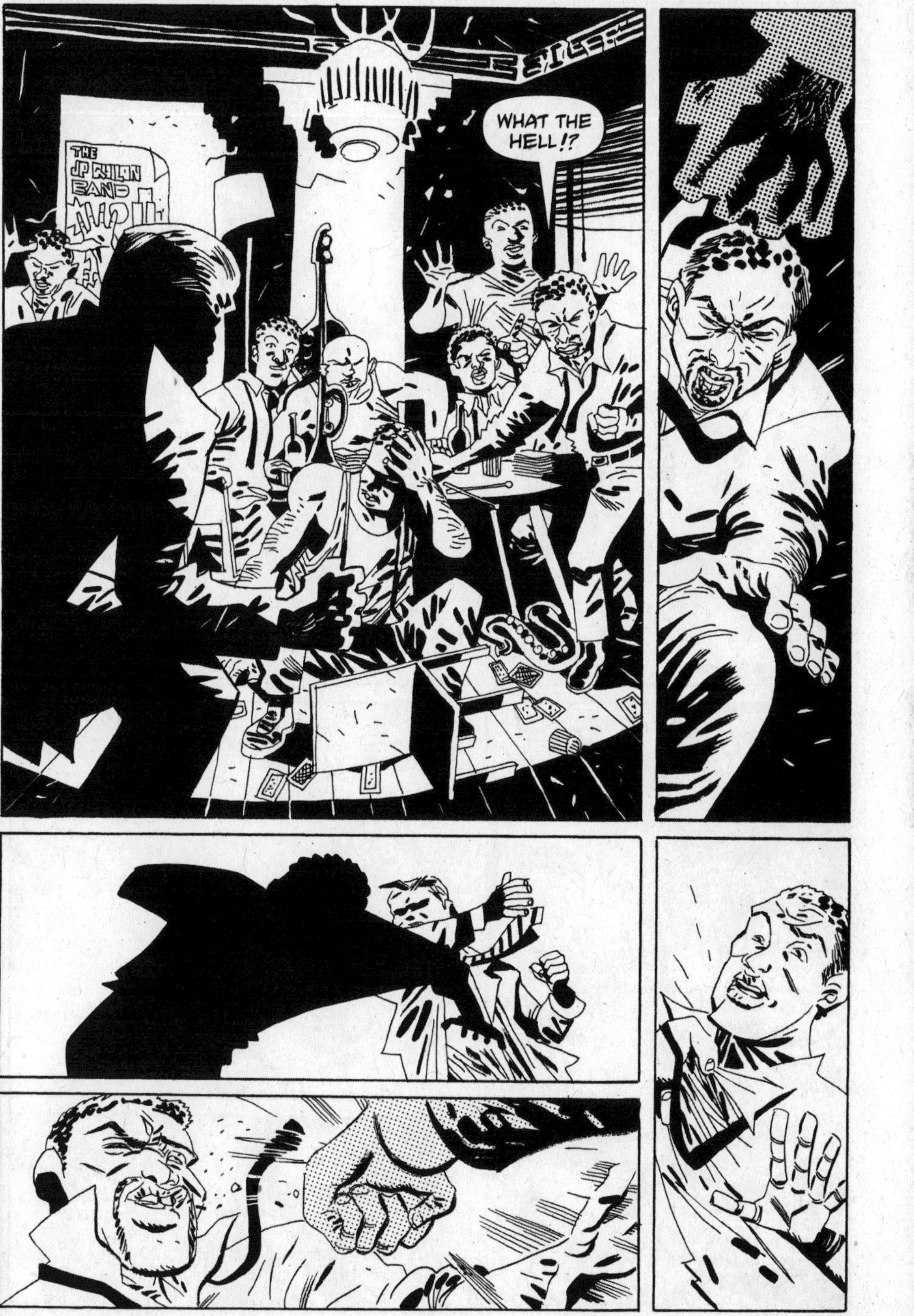
WHAT THE HELL!?

SMASH

WHAT THE FUCK YOU TRYIN' TO DO--GET US ALL ARRESTED!?

HE AIN'T THE HEAT. I SEEN HIM BEFORE IN THE *CLUB.* ONE A' THEM RICH BOYS.

GIT 'IM UP.

WHERE'S SALLY?

HE TOL' YOU-- SHE AIN'T *HERE.*

SHE TOL' ME SHE *WAS.*

YOU GONNA BE COOL?

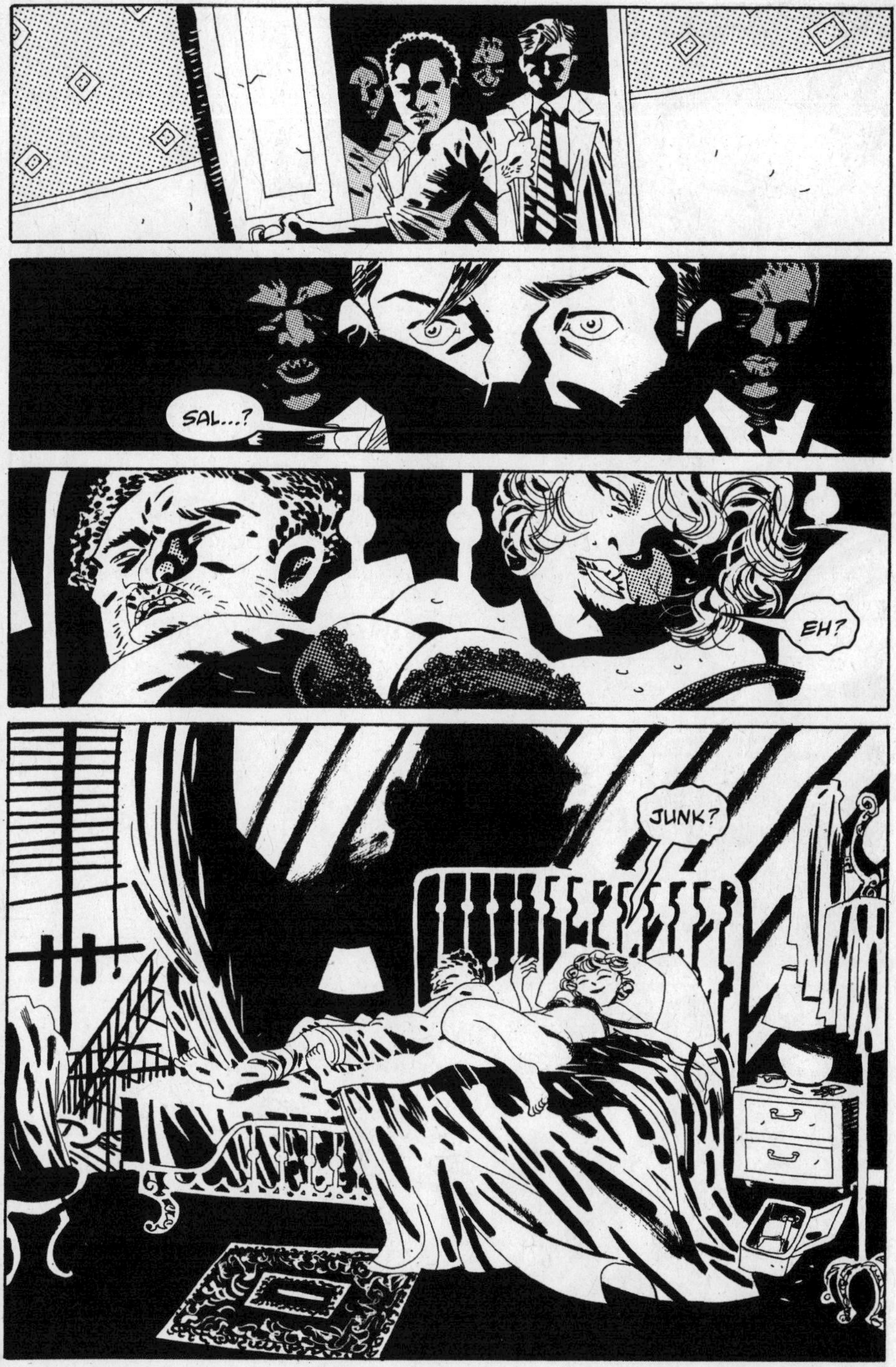
SAL...?
EH?
JUNK?

SORRY 'BOUT, Y'KNOW, BEFORE...

MISS PETRI DIN' SAY THERE'D BE SOMEBODY COMIN' 'ROUN' FOR HER. SHE USUALLY *DOES.*

DEXTER, SOME COFFEE.

ON IT.

SO'S SHE GOT A *GIG* TONIGHT THEN, HUH? MIGHT BE A GOOD NIGHT FOR THE *UNDER-STUDY,* IF Y'KNOW WHAT I MEAN...

NO, NO, NO. MY *PUBLIC...* I'LL BE FINE.

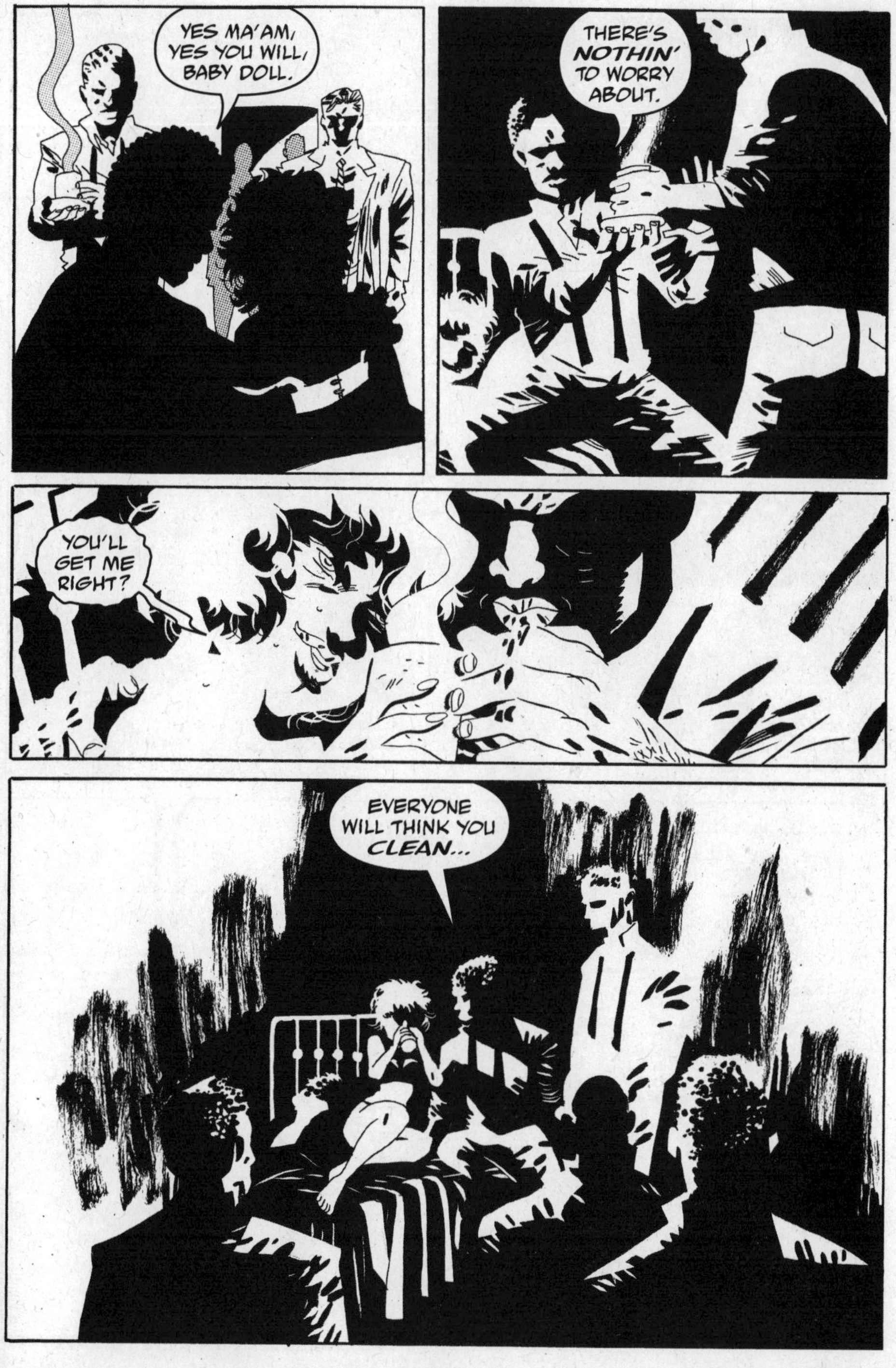
YES MA'AM, YES YOU WILL, BABY DOLL.
THERE'S NOTHIN' TO WORRY ABOUT.
YOU'LL GET ME RIGHT?
EVERYONE WILL THINK YOU CLEAN...

NO, NOT EVERYONE.

NOT ANYONE.

AIN'T *NOBODY* CLEAN. NOBODY.

EVERY-ONE IS *DIRTY.*

THEY'RE ALL LIKE *ME.*

JUNK?

WHERE'VE YOU BEEN?

NOWHERE.

WHAT? YOU *CAN'T* GO *NOWHERE.* NO MATTER WHAT YOU THINK, YOU'RE ALWAYS *SOMEWHERE.*

I'M HERE.

SO AM I.

WE MADE LOVE.

OR WE *STRUGGLED* TO. WHILE WHISPERING AND PANTING... PLANNING OUR *ESCAPE*...

WE HELD ON, DIGGING OUR FINGERS INTO EACH OTHER LIKE WE WERE TRYING TO CRAWL OUT OF A GRAVE.

IT WAS A *HELL* OF A NIGHT. THE *BEST* KIND OF HELL...

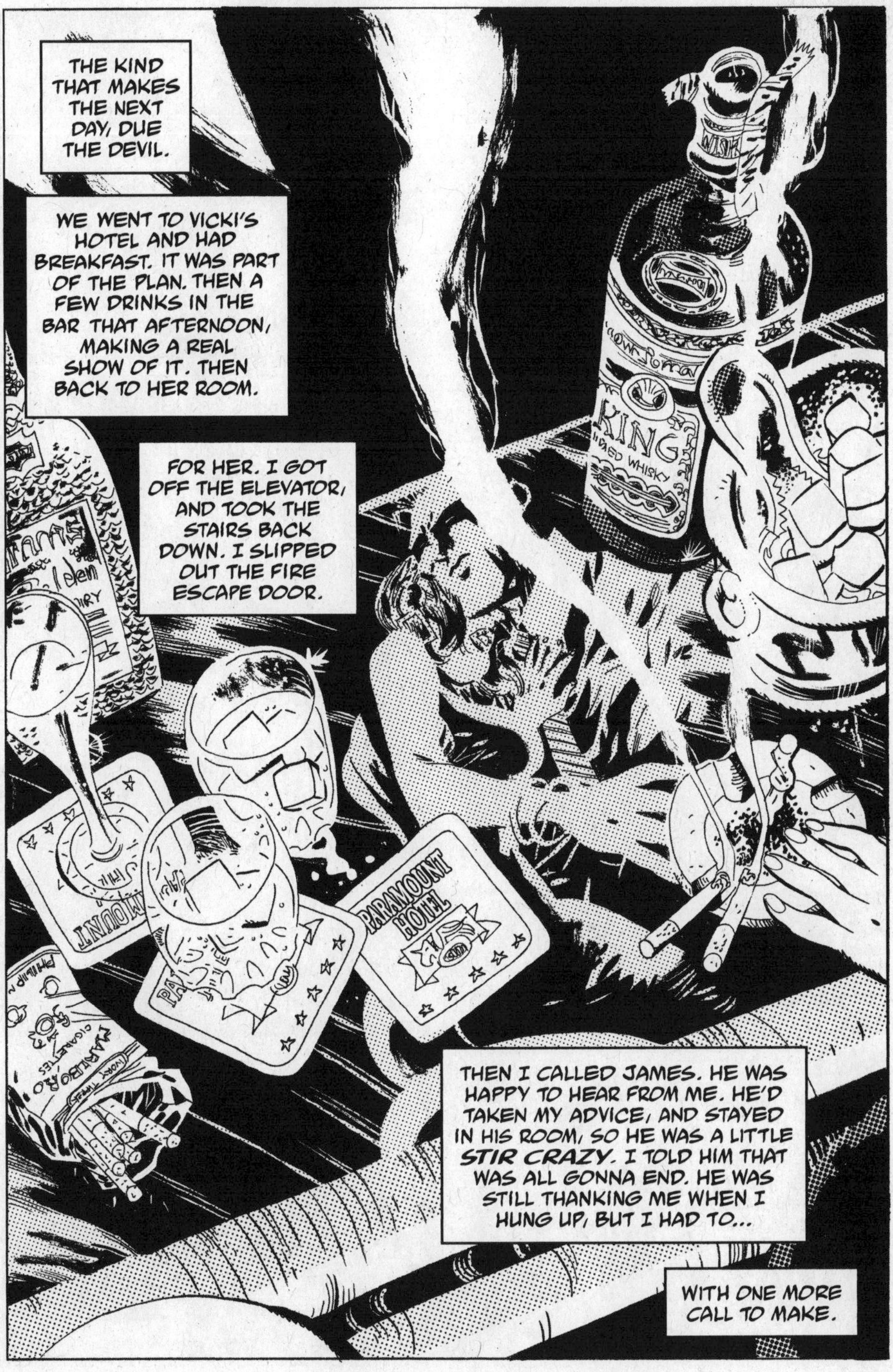
THE KIND THAT MAKES THE NEXT DAY, DUE THE DEVIL.
WE WENT TO VICKI'S HOTEL AND HAD BREAKFAST. IT WAS PART OF THE PLAN. THEN A FEW DRINKS IN THE BAR THAT AFTERNOON, MAKING A REAL SHOW OF IT. THEN BACK TO HER ROOM.
FOR HER. I GOT OFF THE ELEVATOR, AND TOOK THE STAIRS BACK DOWN. I SLIPPED OUT THE FIRE ESCAPE DOOR.
KING
WHISKY
PARAMOUNT HOTEL
THEN I CALLED JAMES. HE WAS HAPPY TO HEAR FROM ME. HE'D TAKEN MY ADVICE, AND STAYED IN HIS ROOM, SO HE WAS A LITTLE STIR CRAZY. I TOLD HIM THAT WAS ALL GONNA END. HE WAS STILL THANKING ME WHEN I HUNG UP, BUT I HAD TO...
WITH ONE MORE CALL TO MAKE.

AFTER THAT I HAD TIME. TIME TO...

I WENT AND HAD A COUPLE OF DRINKS IN A PLACE I'D NEVER BEEN BEFORE. HALFWAY THROUGH THE SECOND ONE I REALIZED I SHOULDN'T BE ANYWHERE, SO I BOUGHT A BOTTLE...

AND I WAITED.

THEN I WATCHED. A BUNCH OF SAD SONS OF BITCHES, HAPPY TO BE DONE WITH WORK FOR THE DAY. TOO STUPID TO REALIZE THAT TOMORROW WOULD BE THE SAME DAY.

SOEFFER CAR DEALERSHIP

THAT MADE ME HAPPY. KNOWING THAT FOR ME, TOMORROW WAS REALLY TOMORROW.

BEFORE THAT, THOUGH, I HAD *TONIGHT.*

NINE-THIRTY. VICKI SHOULD BE ORDERING ROOM SERVICE FOR TWO ABOUT NOW.

KNOCK KNOCK

HELLO, JUNK.

MR. SOEFFER.

C'MON IN.

I MUST SAY, I WAS A BIT **SURPRISED** TO HEAR FROM **YOU** TODAY.

GLAD YOU STAYED ON THE **JOB.**

IT'S BEEN MY **PLEASURE,** SIR.

≥SIGH≤... WELL, I'M NOT **SURE** ABOUT THAT. VICKI, IS SHE...?

LITTLE BIT WORSE FOR THE WEAR, BUT SHE'S OKAY.

THAT'S GOOD TO KNOW. SHE'S MY **DAUGHTER,** BUT WE DON'T ALWAYS SEE EYE TO EYE.

THAT'S AN INTERESTING CHOICE OF WORDS, CONSIDERING.

CONSIDERING *WHAT?*

HMM. DON'T TRY TO BE CUTE, JUNK. IT DOESN'T SUIT YOU.

WHAT DO YOU MEAN BY THAT?

YOU'RE NOT HARD TO FIGURE OUT. I'VE ALWAYS SAID, NINETY-NINE POINT NINE PERCENT OF SALES IS KNOWING WHO IT IS YOU'RE SELLING *TO.*

I'M AFRAID I DON'T *FOLLOW*, SIR.

SALES IS ALL ABOUT CREATING A *NEED.*

THAT'S *ALL* IT IS. A GOOD SALESMAN COULD SELL *RUBBERS* TO A *EUNUCH.*

I DON'T NEED RUBBERS, MR. SOEFFER.

≥SIGH≤... YOU'RE MISSING THE POINT. YOU'RE A DIRECT KIND OF MAN--IT'S YOUR **STRENGTH**. DON'T TRY TO BE SOMETHING ELSE. YOU UNDERSTAND THAT?

YOU CALLED ME TODAY, AND SAID YOU NEEDED TO GET **PAID**. SO, ONE WEEK'S SALARY?

PLUS COMMISSION.

ALL RIGHT. NOW YOUR AVERAGE WAS...

I'M LOOKING FOR *MEECH'S*.

WHO ISN'T? JERRY--HE DOES OKAY BY HIMSELF. DEAL?

I'LL TAKE THAT.

GOOD. VERY GOOD. SEE HOW EASY, GETTING WHAT YOU WANTED ALL ALONG?

JUST TRUST YOURSELF-- LIKE I DO.

YOU DO TRUST YOURSELF, SIR. MAYBE TOO MUCH.

...

NO JUNK, I MEANT I TRUST YOU.

NOW, I KNOW I REACTED HARSHLY THE MORNING AFTER THE HORRIBLE INCIDENT AT THAT PARTY...

MAYBE SAID SOME THINGS I *SHOULDN'T* HAVE.

I GUESS MY PROBLEM WAS THE WAY YOU HANDLED THE SITUATION--WHICH IS UNFAIR--*I'M* NOT THE ONE THAT *FOUND* THAT POOR BOY'S BODY.

BUT YOU *DID* HANDLE IT-- YOUR WAY. AND I'M GRATEFUL, SON.

AND PROTECTIVE OF MY LITTLE *GIRL.*

SHE'S NOT SO LITTLE *ANYMORE.*

I BET SHE REMINDS YOU OF YOUR *WIFE,* HUH?

VICKI? NO. BEING AT *HOME* MADE MARIE HAPPY-- COOKING, DIGGING IN THE GARDEN...

I WISH VICKI *WERE* MORE LIKE HER MOTHER. MY PROBLEM IS SHE TOOK AFTER *ME,* ALWAYS CHASING...

THAT DOESN'T GET YOU ANYTHING IN THE END.

IT GOT YOU *THIS.*

AND THIS IS *HERS.* BUT IT'S NOT ENOUGH.

I WANT WHAT *ANY* FATHER DOES--TO BE A *GRANDFATHER.*

I WANT MY DAUGHTER TO MEET A NICE BOY WHO MAKES HER HAPPY. SETTLE *DOWN.*

WHAT IF SHE *HAS?*

YOU MEAN YOU?

I'M NOT THE ONE THAT CALLED ME SON.

HEH.

HA.

HAHA... OH, VICKI. JUNK, JUNK...

HAHAHAHAHA--

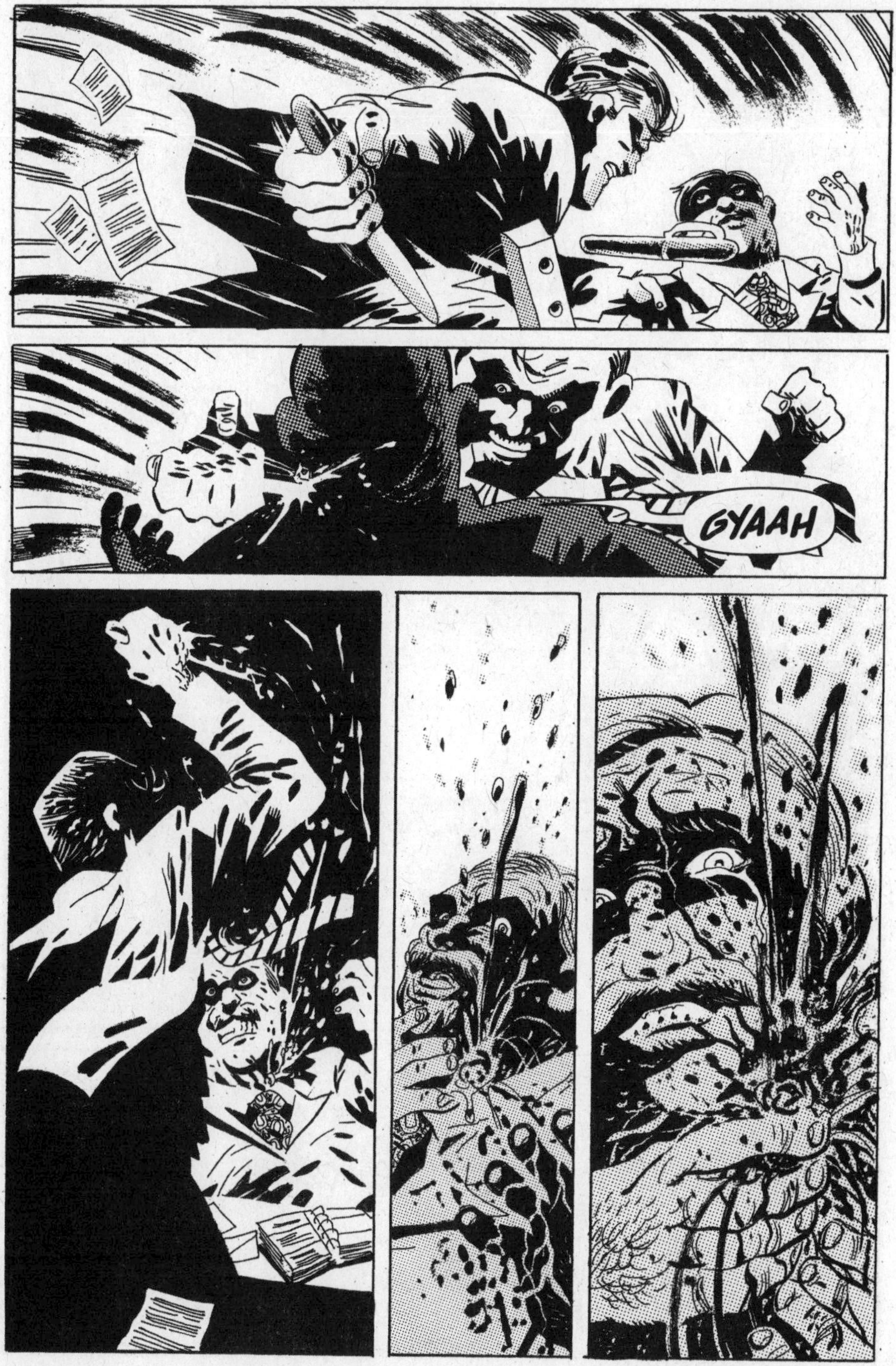
GYAAH

NINE FORTY-FIVE. DINNER'S BEING DELIVERED.

VICKI IS ASKING THE BELL HOP IF HE CAN KEEP MINE *WARM*, BECAUSE "MY BOYFRIEND, HE HAD TO STEP OUT FOR A MINUTE, ON BUSINESS."

TEN O'CLOCK.

JUNK?

IN THE CAR, JAMES.

MAN, I'M *COLD.* YOU COLD?

NO. I'M *NOT.*

SO...IT'S SET *UP,* LIKE YOU *SAID* IT WAS?

...IT'S SET UP.

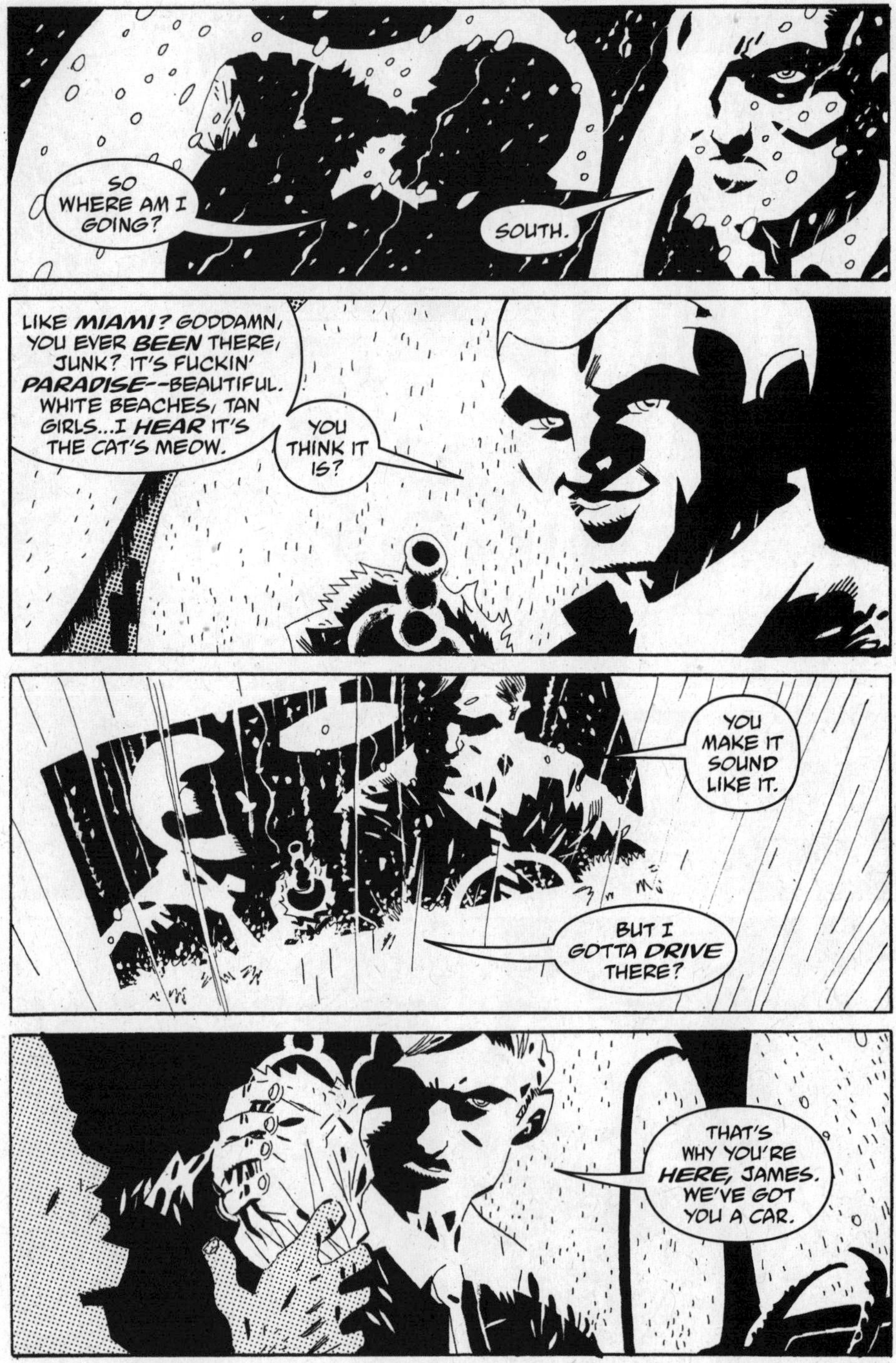
SO WHERE AM I GOING?
SOUTH.
LIKE MIAMI? GODDAMN, YOU EVER BEEN THERE, JUNK? IT'S FUCKIN' PARADISE--BEAUTIFUL. WHITE BEACHES, TAN GIRLS...I HEAR IT'S THE CAT'S MEOW.
YOU THINK IT IS?
YOU MAKE IT SOUND LIKE IT.
BUT I GOTTA DRIVE THERE?
THAT'S WHY YOU'RE HERE, JAMES. WE'VE GOT YOU A CAR.

THAT'S GREAT. *REALLY* GREAT.

JUNK?

I JUST WANT TO SAY, I APPRECIATE WHAT YOU'RE *DOING* FOR ME. STICKING YOUR NECK OUT, I DON'T THINK I'D DO THE SAME FOR YOU.

SCRATCH THAT--I *WOULD* NOW-- *DEFINITELY.* YOU'VE SORT OF CHANGED MY OPINION ABOUT SOME THINGS.

JAMES, *DON'T...*

I'M SERIOUS. MY *"TRUE"* FRIENDS--THEY'RE JUST A CROWD, IF YOU KNOW WHAT I MEAN.

I KNOW HOW A CROWD CAN *TURN* ON YOU...

YEAH-- YEAH, *EXACTLY*. YOU, OF ALL PEOPLE. THE *GOOD* LIFE, JUST WAITING... THEN THAT SCANDAL... AND THE INJURY.

I THOUGHT YOU GOT WHAT YOU *DESERVED*.

BUT I KNOW NOW, KNOWING YOU-- *NONE* OF IT WAS TRUE.

YOU GOT A BAD BREAK. JUST LIKE *ME*.

WE SHOULD GO GET THIS *DONE*. THE SOONER YOU'RE GONE, THE *BETTER*.

RIGHT, RIGHT.

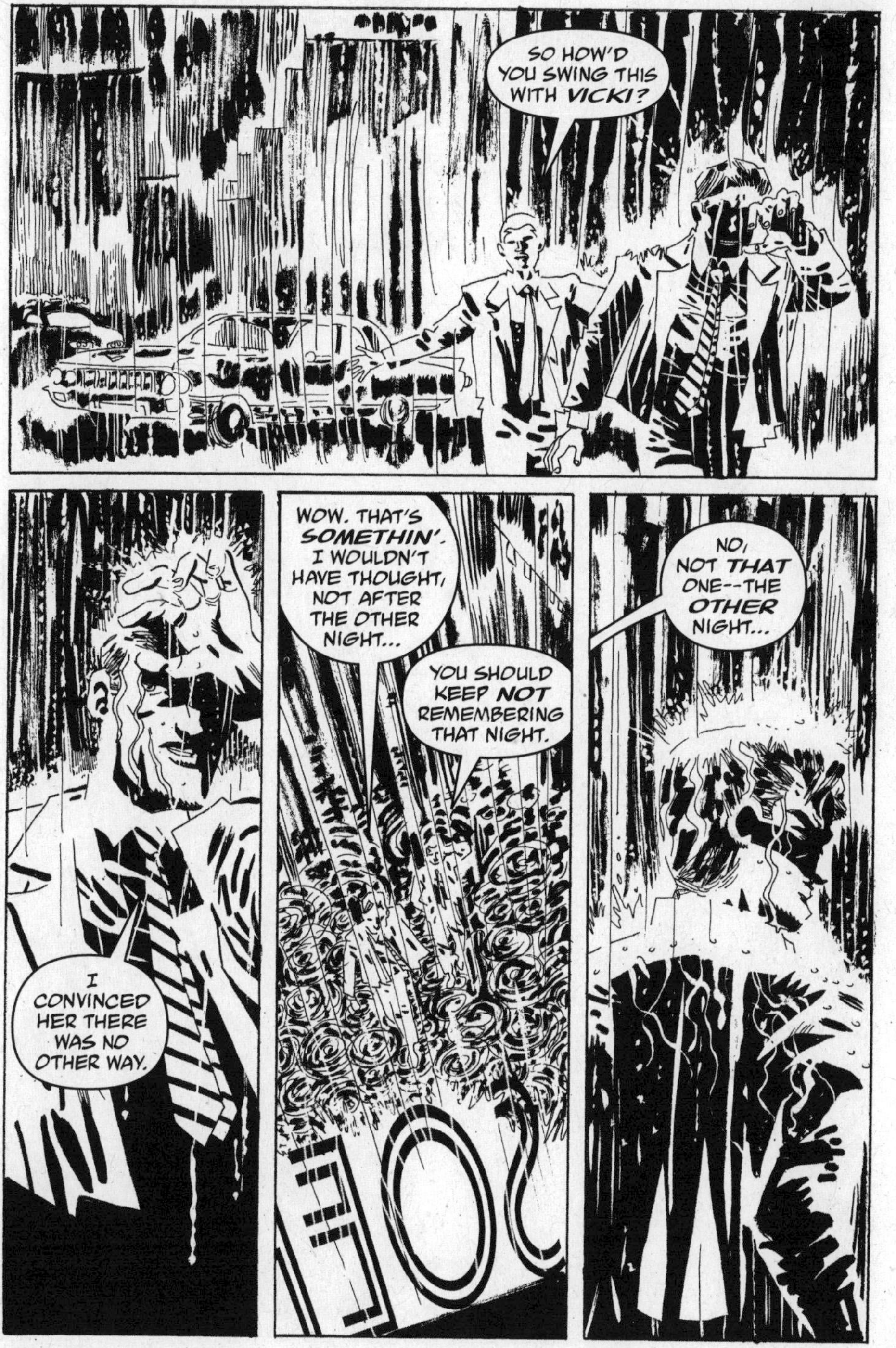
SO HOW'D YOU SWING THIS WITH VICKI?
I CONVINCED HER THERE WAS NO OTHER WAY.
WOW. THAT'S SOMETHIN'. I WOULDN'T HAVE THOUGHT, NOT AFTER THE OTHER NIGHT...
YOU SHOULD KEEP NOT REMEMBERING THAT NIGHT.
NO, NOT THAT ONE--THE OTHER NIGHT...

WHEN I WENT TO SEE *HER*-- *BEFORE* I CAME TO YOU...

...I TRIED TO TELL HER THERE WAS NO *WAY* I KILLED KENNY...HE WAS MY *FRIEND*, AND I WOULDN'T DO THAT, NO MATTER *WHAT* HE PULLED...

WHEN SHE SAID SHE WASN'T AWARE HOW "FRIENDLY" KENNY AND I *REALLY* WERE...

AND LAUGHED, CALLING ME A...WELL, I *LOST* IT.

I'M SORRY I *HIT* HER. SHE'S OKAY, RIGHT?

YEAH. VICKI'S OKAY.

SHE'S GOOD.

CAR DEALERSH

I GOT A **GOING AWAY** PRESENT FOR YOU, JAMES...

WHAT'S THIS?

WHAT'S IT **LOOK** LIKE?

A KNIFE.

IT'S A LETTER OPENER.

IT **LOOKS** LIKE A KNIFE.

JAMES... YOU'RE **WRONG** ABOUT ME.

I DID IT.

WHAT THEY **SAID.** BACK IN COLLEGE, AT **NOTRE DAME.**

SOME GUYS FROM CHICAGO...MOBBED-UP TOUGH GUYS. WHAT THEY OFFERED WAS GOOD--CONSIDERING I WASN'T MAKING *NO* DOUGH AT THE TIME.

JUST MISS SOME BIG TACKLES, KEEP THE SCORE *CLOSE...*

I WAS A THREE-TIME ALL-AMERICAN. I DIDN'T GIVE A FUCK ABOUT NO SPREAD. I HAD FUCKING PRIDE--A LOVE FOR THE GAME--*FUCK* THE GAMBLERS.

AND WE DIDN'T LOSE.

I MEAN, OTHER THAN *ME.*

I NEVER GOT PAID. WHEN THE FEDS...THOSE TOUGH GUYS *ROLLED OVER.*

IT ALL CAME OUT, AFTER I WAS DRAFTED...YOU WOULDA THOUGHT I HAD GODDAMN *LEPROSY.*

THE REST OF THE JERK-OFFS ON THE TEAM, THEY WOULDN'T EVEN *SPEAK* TO ME...

EVEN AFTER NOTHING WAS PROVEN.

DIDN'T MATTER THAT I HAD MORE *TALENT* THAN *ANY* OF 'EM. THOUGHT I WAS GUILTY. PROLLY 'CAUSE THEY'D ALL DONE THE SAME, ONE TIME OR ANOTHER.

I SHOULDN' A EVEN BEEN *PLAYING* IN THAT LAST PRE-SEASON GAME...

I WAS A STARTER-- THE BEST PLAYER ON THAT DEFENSE--AS A *ROOKIE!*

THAT HIT ON MY KNEE...THERE HAD TO BE A FUCKIN' BOUNTY. A *CHEAP SHOT...*

I BEEN *PAYIN'* FOR EVERY DAY SINCE.

...WHY YOU TELLING THIS TO *ME?*

JAMES, YOU'RE THE RIGHT *GUY*, AT THE RIGHT *TIME*, IN THE RIGHT *PLACE.*

I CAN *CONFIDE* IN YOU.

VICKI'S WAITING.

C'MON.

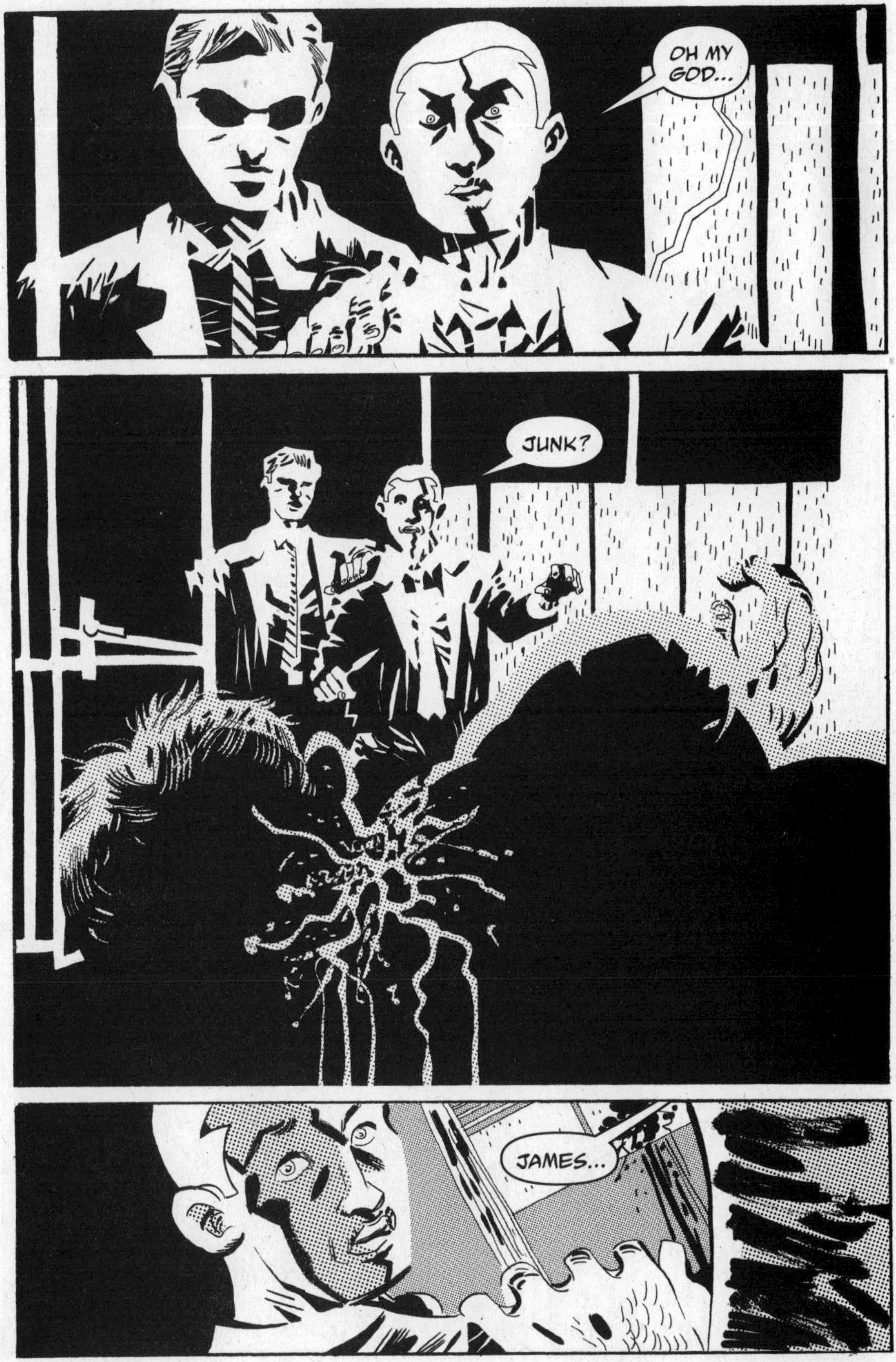
OH MY GOD...
JUNK?
JAMES...

IT'S TOO LATE TO TURN BACK.

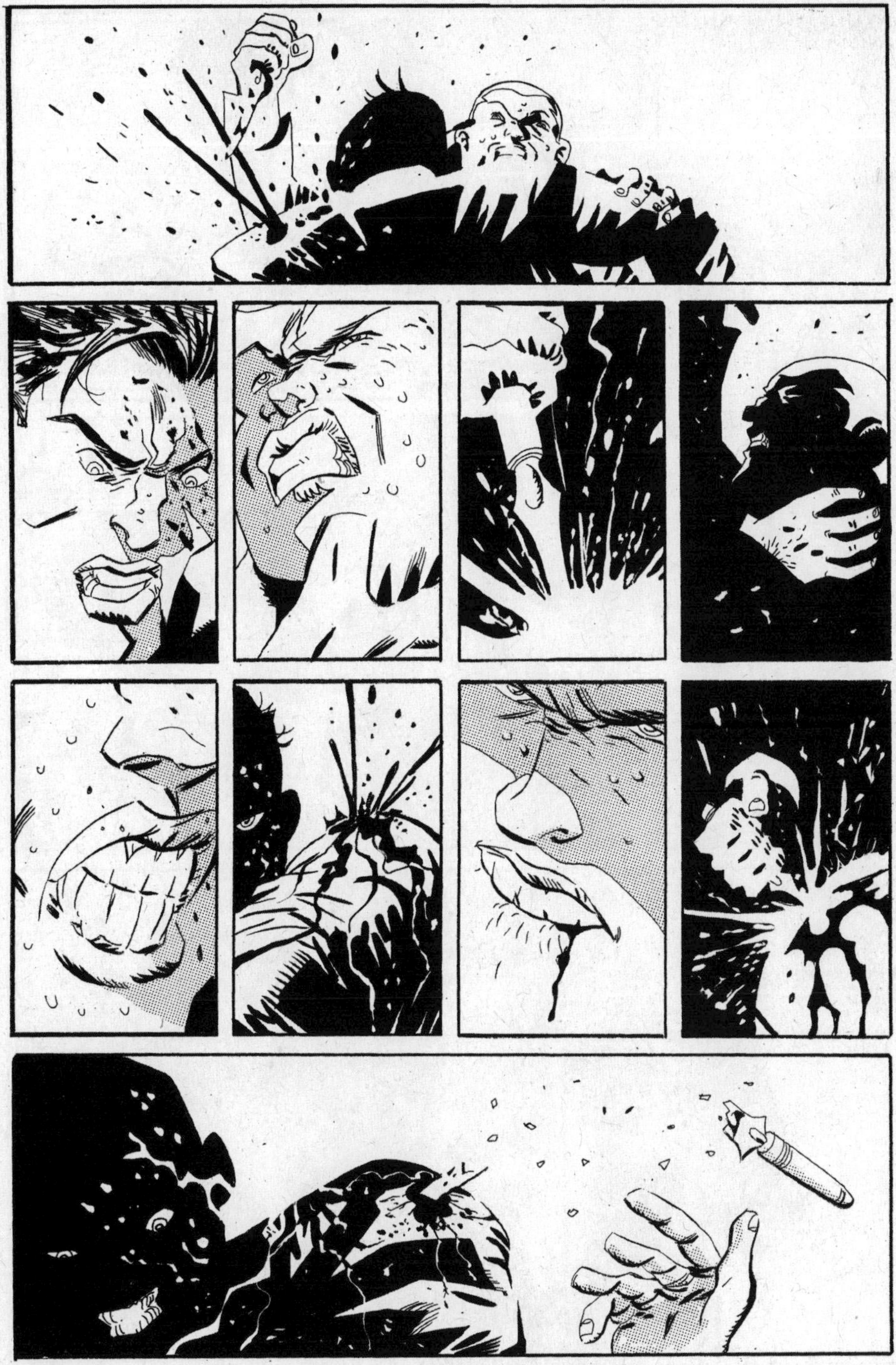

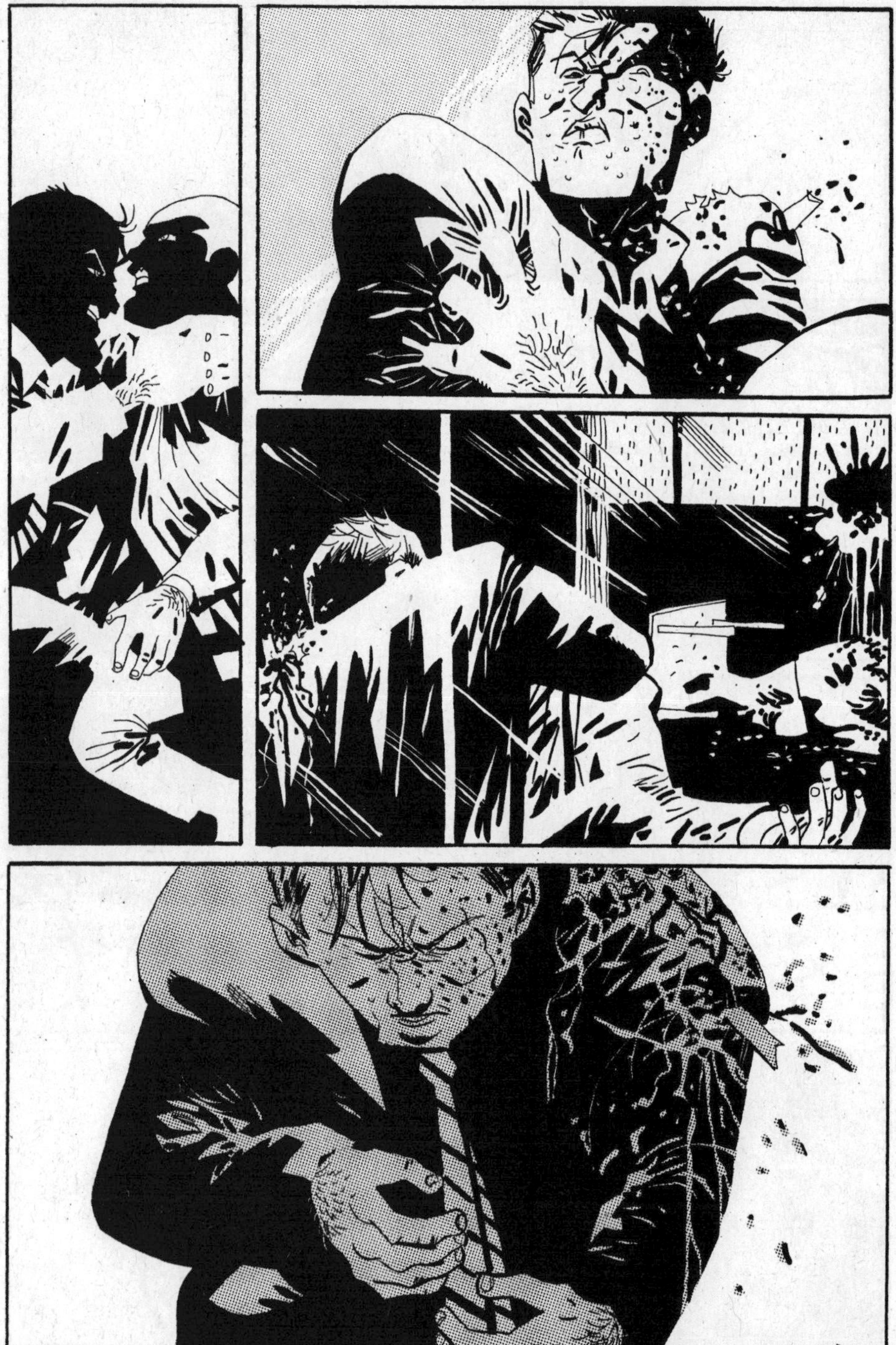

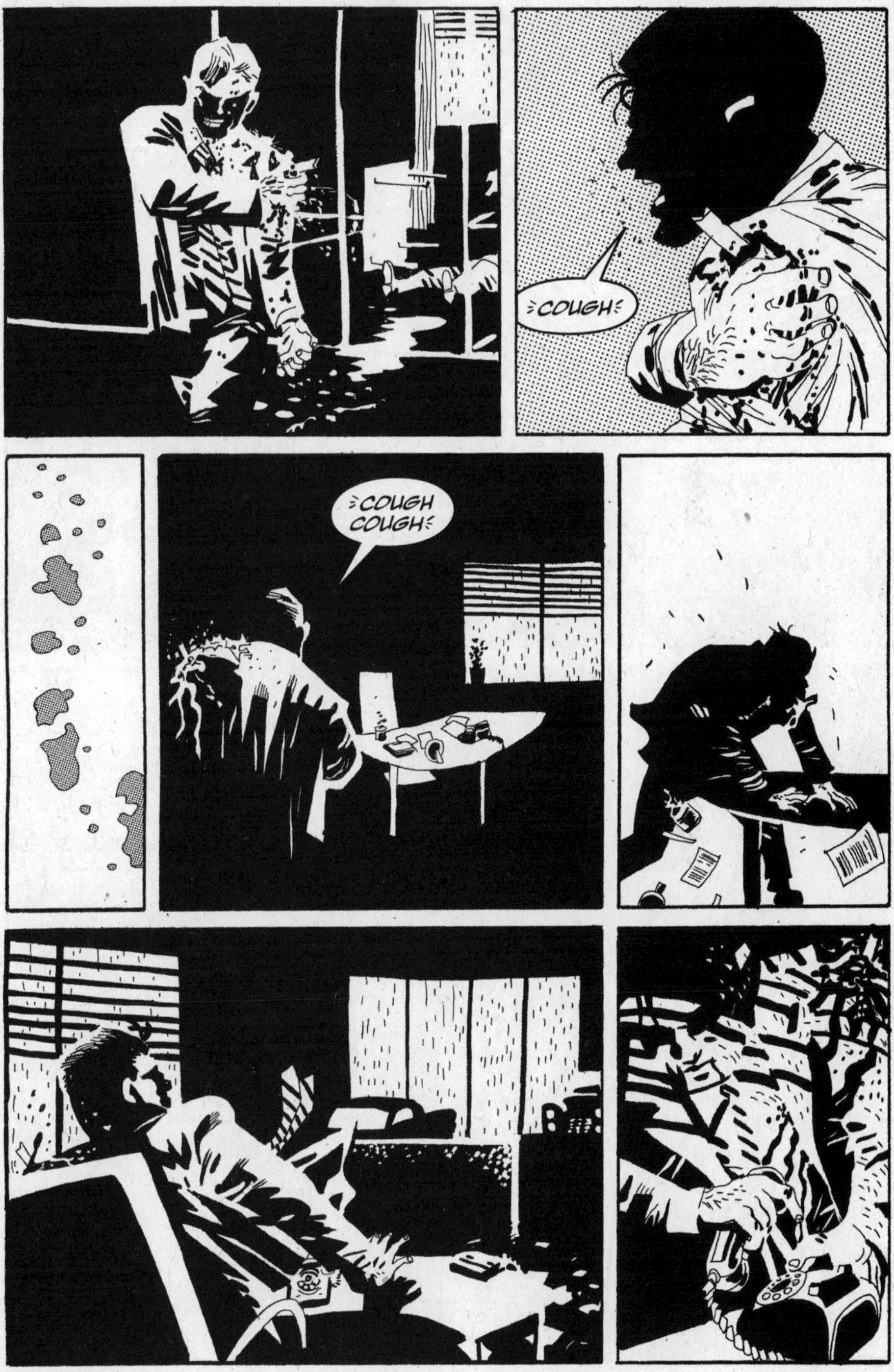
COUGH
COUGH COUGH

RING
RING

NUMBER, PLEASE?

OPERATOR...

GET ME THE POLICE...

I WOKE UP IN THE HOSPITAL. THE DOCTOR SAID I WAS *LUCKY*. I DIDN'T BOTHER TO CORRECT HIM.

THE COPS ASKED ME SOME QUESTIONS, LIKE WHAT WAS I DOING THERE AT THAT TIME OF NIGHT, BUT IT WAS *ROUTINE...*

THEY'D ALREADY FOUND MY ALIBI-- MADE OUT TO ME ON SOEFFER'S DESK--AND THE *MURDER WEAPON* IN JAMES' HAND.

I'D SHOWN UP TO PICK UP MY CHECK. I WALKED IN, AND FOUND MR. SOEFFER DEAD, AND JAMES-- HE MUST HAVE BEEN TRYING TO STEAL A *CAR...*

HE CAME AT ME--YOU SHOULD HAVE SEEN HIS EYES! HE WAS CRAZY--KILL HAPPY... WHAT *ELSE* WAS I SUPPOSED TO DO?

JUST LIKE WE--SHE--HAD PLANNED. SURE, I HAD A *PART* IN IT...

IT WAS THE *PERFECT* CRIME. OR SHOULD I SAY...

...*VICKI* WAS PERFECT.

SHE DIDN'T STICK TO THE *PLAN*.

RATHER THAN STAY AT THE HOTEL TO MAKE MY ALIBI AIRTIGHT, SHE WENT OUT THAT NIGHT, AND DID WHAT SHE HAD TO DO TO MAKE THE *PAPERS* I READ THE NEXT MORNING.

I SUPPOSE I CAN'T FAULT HER FOR THAT. I DIDN'T STICK TO IT EITHER.

I MEAN, I WAS SUPPOSED TO LET JAMES STAB ME ONCE, THEN *REALLY* APPLY THE PRESSURE...

DON'T KNOW WHY I COULDN'T BRING MYSELF TO DO THAT.

REGARDLESS, MY TOMORROW HAD COME. VICKI THOUGH, WAS A *NO SHOW.*

WHEN I GOT OUT OF THE HOSPITAL, I WENT TO SEE HER. SHE HAD TAKEN OVER HER FATHER'S BUSINESS BY THEN, AND I FIGURED AT THE LEAST, SHE *OWED* ME.

I *TOLD* HER AS MUCH. SHE AGREED.

THEN *LAUGHED* AT ME.

...IT'S BECOME A SOUND I'VE GOTTEN *USED* TO.

I'M
WAITING...

SORRY, MISS
SOEFFER.

WAITING.
SO AM I.

VICKI, AS
PERFECT AS
SHE IS?...

SHE
WON'T LAST
FOREVER--
NOTHING
PERFECT
EVER
DOES.

JUST
GIVE ME A
CHANCE...

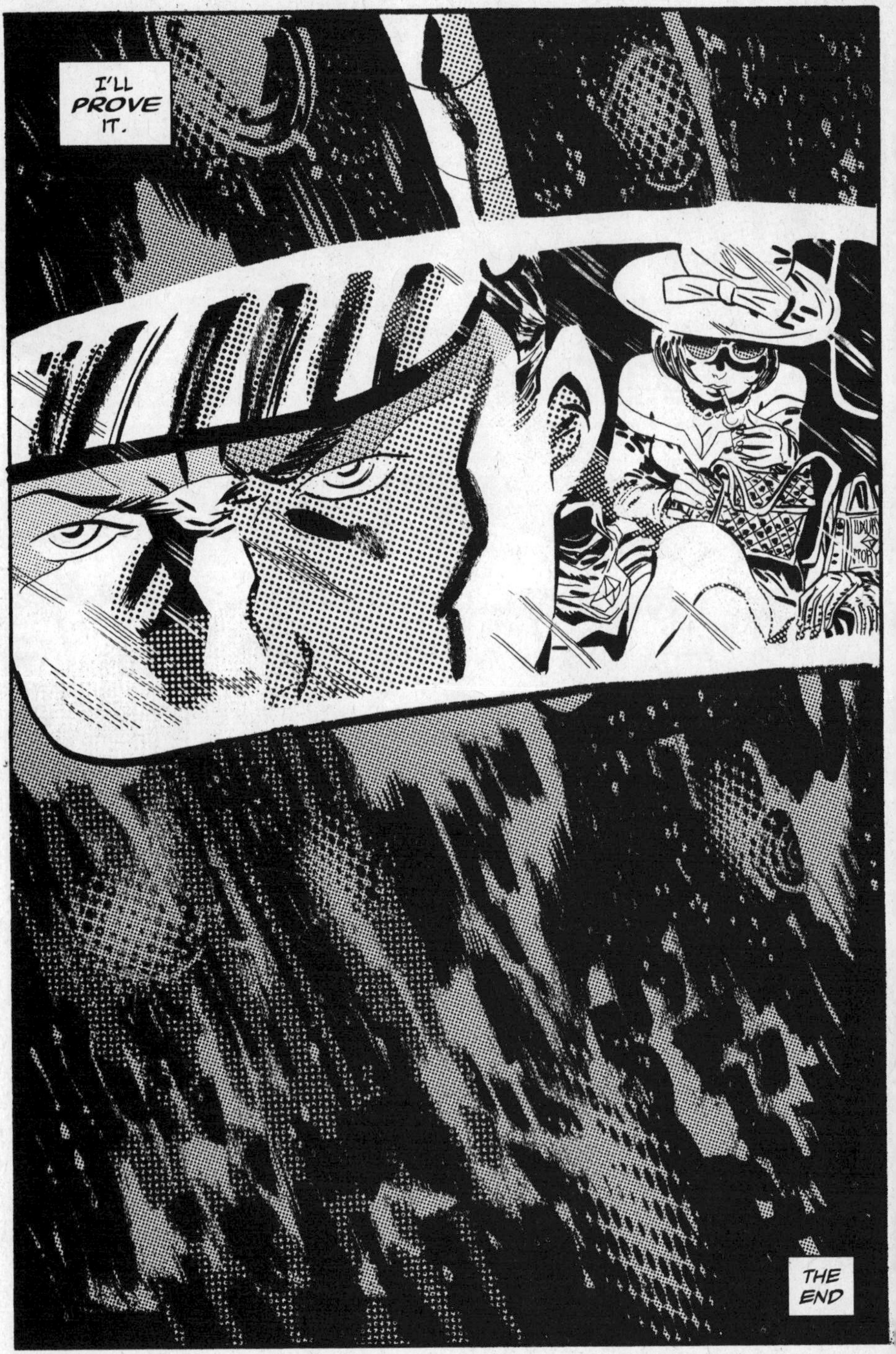
I'LL PROVE IT.
THE END